PROOF
of the
Illuminati

Other books from the *Invisible College Press:*

Classic Non-fiction:
The Rosicrucian Manuscripts, edited by Benedict J. Williamson

Classic Fiction:
Wieland, by Charles Brockden Brown

Contemporary Non-fiction:
UFO Politics at the White House, by Larry W. Bryant

Contemporary Fiction:
Leeward, by D. Edward Bradley
The Third Day, by Mark Graham
Cold in the Light, by Charles Gramlich
Phase Two, by C. Scott Littleton
Marsface, by R. M. Pala
City of Pillars, by Dominic Peloso
Utopian Reality, by Catherine Simone

Classic Technical Works:
A Treatise of Mathematical Instruments, by John Robertson
The Practical Surveyor, by Samuel Wyld

For more details, visit http://www.invispress.com.

PROOF

of the

Illuminati

the 1802 Edition by
Seth Payson, A. M.

Containing an Abstract of the Most Interesting
Parts of What DR. ROBISON and the ABBE BARRUEL
have Published on this Subject; with Collateral
Proofs and General Observations

The Invisible College Press
Arlington, Virginia

Proof of the Illuminati

Original printed by Samuel Etheridge for Seth Payson, A. M., in 1802

ISBN: 1-931468-14-1

First Printing

Published by
The Invisible College Press, LLC
P. O. Box 209
Woodbridge, Virginia 22194-0209
http://www.invispress.com

Please send questions and comments to
editor@invispress.com

———— Here nature breeds
Perverse, all monstrous, all prodigious things
Abominable, unutterable, and worse
Than fables yet have feign'd or fear conceiv'd.
— MILTON

Contents

Forward

T H I S work, *Proof of the Illuminati*, was first published in 1802 under the longer title *Proofs of the Real Existence, and Dangerous Tendency, of Illuminism*. It was printed in Charlestown, Massachusetts by Samuel Etheridge for the author, Seth Payson.

Reverend Seth Payson, D. D. was born in 1758 and died in 1820. He, like his father, Rev. Phillips Payson, and several of his brothers, became a Congregational preacher. After graduating from Harvard, he was appointed as the minister of the Congregational church in Rindge, New Hampshire in 1782, and held this post for the rest of his life. At least one of his sons also followed him into the ministry.

Payson was very active in establishing new churches for communities in northern New England, including the church in Coventry, Vermont. He was the author of numerous sermons, several of which were published and had a modest distribution. Additionally, Payson helped educate and provide for Sophia Sawyer, a woman who would later become famous for establishing the Fayetteville Female Academy.

Rev. Payson served in the New Hampshire State senate from 1802-1805. He was a staunch Federalist supporter. Along with its alarming message regarding both religion and state, *Proof of the Illuminati* was also a part of Payson's campaign platform.

The Invisible College Press is pleased to once again provide this valuable work to the public.

Preface

T H E efforts which have been made to discredit the existence of Illuminism, and the torrents of abuse which have been so liberally poured on such as have attempted, apparently from the purest motives, to unveil this mystery of iniquity, have in part produced the end designed. Some have mistaken vociferation for argument, and confident assertions for proofs; while others have been prevented from publishing their beliefs and their fears, not choosing to encounter the shafts of ridicule and defamation; weapons found to be of great importance in this *age of reason*. A general stupor has hence taken place of that just alarm, occasioned by the first discovery of this infernal combination.

But has the cause of alarm ceased? There has been much clamor indeed, but have any solid, satisfying proofs been exhibited, either that there has not been, or is not now existing, a conspiracy, which has for its ultimate object, the abolition of Christianity and government? Solid proofs alone ought to satisfy us on a subject so highly interesting to mankind. Such proofs have not, I confess, come to my knowledge. Recent events do, on the contrary, confirm my belief, that a systematical attempt is now in operation to undermine the foundation of every religious, moral, and social establishment. To those who have this belief, it must appear important that the impending danger be placed in the most conspicuous point of view; that the evidence of this fact, now diffused through expensive and voluminous tracts, and arising from a variety of circumstances, should be collected into one point, freed from the obscurity in which it has been industriously involved, and the whole comprised in a volume, easy to the purchaser, and intelligible to every reader. The importance of such a publication at the present critical period, and which I have expected, and hoped to see from some abler hand, is all the apology I have to offer for undertaking the task.

To defend religion, by exposing plots concerted for its destruction, is the principal object of this publication: and if any thing of a political nature is introduced, it is with a view of detecting, and counteracting that dark policy, which has connected the subversion of every good government, with the overthrow of Christianity.

I claim no merit for discovering what I could not avoid seeing, but by shutting my eyes; and I fear no censure, for I have obeyed the call of duty. I have no hope of convincing those who have had access to the evidence here referred to, but for reasons best known to themselves, have rejected it; nor the many who have presumed to give judgement without examination: this statement of evidence is for those who have no medium of vision; and those, whose optics have been injured by the dust which sophistry, prejudice, and the powers of darkness have raised. Could I contribute but a mite, which is my all, to preserve my country from that vortex of anarchy, which has engulfed the liberties, civil and religious, and the peace, property, and lives of millions, my labor will not be unrewarded.

Preliminary Observations

T O remove the obstructions which prejudiced and designing men have raised, is often a necessary, but laborious and ungrateful task, attending our inquiries after truth. No sooner is the precious gem brought to view, than its enemies, who hate its light, and cannot endure its brilliancy, and busily employed in covering it with filth and rubbish; hence much of the labor of those who wish to posses the heavenly boon.

The testimony of Professor Robison, and Abbe Barruel, would doubtless have been considered as ample, in any case which did not interest the prejudices and passions of men against them. The scurrility and odium with which they have been loaded is perfectly natural, and what the nature of their testimony would have led anyone to expect. Men will endeavor to invalidate that evidence which tends to unveil their dark designs: and it cannot be expected that those who believe that "the end sanctifies the means," will be very scrupulous as to their measures. Certainly he was not, who invented the following character, and arbitrarily applied it to Dr. Robison, which might have been applied with as much propriety to any other person in Europe or America. The character here referred to, is taken from the American Mercury, printed at Hartford, Sept. 26, 1799, by E. Babcock. In this paper, on the pretended authority of

Professor Ebeling,* we are told, "That Robison had lived too fast for his income, and to supply deficiencies, had undertaken to alter a bank bill; that he was detected, and fled to France; that having been expelled the Lodge in Edinburgh, he applied in France for the second grade, but was refused; that he made the same attempt in Germany, and afterwards in Russia, but never succeeded; and from this entertained the bitterest hatred to Masonry; that after wandering about Europe, for two years, by writing to secretary Dundas, and presenting a copy of his book, which, it was judged, would answer certain purposes of the ministry, the prosecution against him was stopped, the Professor returned in triumph to his country, and now lives upon a handsome pension, instead of suffering the same fate of his predecessor Dodd."

A writer in the *National Intelligencer,* of Jan. 1801, who styles himself "A friend to the Truth," and from whom, (if conjecture has pointed out the real author) better things ought to be expected, speaks of Dr. Robinson as "a man distinguished by abject dependence on a party; by the base crimes of forgery, and adultery; and by frequent paroxysms of insanity."

As Dr. Robison is a principal evidence in the cause now pending, it will be necessary to inquire, whether this is indeed a just view of the man. The result of this inquiry, contrasted with the above character, will serve to give the public some idea of the means which have been made use of

---

* It is but justice to the character of Professor Ebeling, to say, that in none of his Letters to his American Correspondents, of which I have information, has he given the least intimation that Professor Robison was guilty of the crimes here imputed to him. Nor has he, to my knowledge, ever criminated his moral character. These base calumnies originated, not from Mr. Ebeling, but from a spirit or malignant opposition to Dr. Robison; and they furnish strong evidence of the truth of his writings.

to discredit Illuminism, and how *benevolently* disposed
some among us are, to prevent their countrymen from
being misled by what are called, the *ridiculous reveries* of
Robison.   The reader's patience, it is feared, will be exhausted by the detail of credentials which the effrontery of
his accusers have rendered necessary; but the character of a
witness is of the first importance.   The following sketch of
the principal events of the life of Dr. Robison, was drawn up
from authentic documents, received direct from Edinburgh,
through a respectable channel.*

"The father of the Professor, a respectable country
gentleman, intended him for the church, and gave him eight
years of an University education at Glasgow.   Preferring a
different profession, he accepted an offer of going into the
Navy, with very flattering prospects.   He was appointed
Mathematical Instructor to his Royal Highness the Duke of
York.   In that office, he accordingly entered the Navy in
February, 1759, being that day twenty years old.   He was
present at the siege of Quebec.   With the late Admiral
Knowles, he was particularly connected, and his son,
afterwards captain Knowles, one of the most promising
young officers in the British Navy, was committed to his
charge.

"In 1761, he was sent by the board of Admiralty, to
make trial of Harrison's Watch at Jamaica.   At the peace of
1763, he returned to College.   In 1764, he was again appointed by the Admiralty to make trial of Harrison's
improved Watch at Barbados; but his patron, Lord Anson,

---

* Concerning the facts contained in this historical sketch, which were
communicated to Dr. Erskine, he writes thus.   "The most important
facts in it I have had access to know, being first settled at Kirkintillock,
the neighboring parish to Boderoch, where lay the estate of his worthy
father.   For the few facts of which I know less, full and unexceptionable
vouchers can be produced."

being dead, and the conditions not such as pleased him, he declined the employment, returned again to College, and took under his care the only remaining son of his friend, Sir Charles Knowles. This son is the present Admiral Sir Charles Knowles. In 1770, Sir Charles was invited by the Empress of Russia to take charge of her Navy. He took Mr. Robison with him as his Secretary. In 1772, Mr. Robison was appointed superintendent of the education in the Marine Cadet Corps, where he had under his direction about 500 youth, 350 of whom were sons of noblemen and gentlemen, and 26 masters in the different studies. The Academy being burnt, Mr. Robison, with his pupils, removed to an ancient palace of Peter the Great at Cronstadt, a most miserable, desolate island, where, finding no agreeable society, he availed himself of the first opportunity, of quitting so unpleasant a situation, and accepted an invitation from the Magistrates of Edinburgh, to the Professorship of Natural Philosophy in the University in that city, which ranks among the first Universities in the world. To this very honorable office he acceded in August, 1774, and from that time continued his lectures, without interruption, till 1792, when illness obliged him to ask for an assistant. To enable him to give such a salary to his assistant, as would make the place worth the acceptance of a man of talents, the King was pleased to give him a pension of £. 100 a year. After five years confinement, by a painful disorder, he resumed his chair, in 1797.

"In 1786, he was elected a member of the Philosophical Society at Philadelphia, of which Mr. Jefferson is President; and in 1797, a member of the Royal Society of Manchester. In 1799, after the publication of his book, the University of Glasgow, where he received his education, conferred on him, unsolicited, the honor of a Doctor's degree in Law, in which, contrary to the usual custom in these cases, is given a very particular and flattering account of his nine years studies in that University. This peculiar evidence of esteem and respect was given in this way, in order that his Diploma might have all the civil consequences which long standing could give. When he published his book, in 1797, he was Secretary of the Royal Society of Edinburgh. In April, 1800, without solicitation of a single friend, he was unanimously elected a Foreign Member (there are but six) of the Imperial Academy of Sciences, at St. Petersburg, (which, in point of reputation, is esteemed the third on the continent of Europe) in the room of the much lamented and highly celebrated Dr. Black. To prepare for the press, and superintend the publication of the Chemical writings of this great man, required the ablest Chemist in Great Britain. This distinguished honor has been conferred on Professor Robison, who has undertaken this important work. This appointment, for which no man perhaps is more competent, together with the numerous, learned, and copious articles which he has furnished for the Encyclopedia Britannica, fully evince that in reputation and solid learning, he ranks among the first literary characters in Europe. Add to all this, *he sustains a* MORAL *character, so fair and unblemished, that any man may safely be challenged to lay anything to his charge of which an honest man need be ashamed."*

The following account of Professor Robison, is from a Work, entitled, "Literary Memoirs of Living Authors of Great Britain, &c." in two volumes, 8vo, published in London, 1798, for R. Faulder:

"John Robison, Esq. M. A. Secretary to the Royal Society at Edinburgh, and Professor of Natural Philosophy in the University. Professor Robison is distinguished for his accurate and extensive knowledge, especially on subjects of science. He contributed to the Encyclopedia Britannica the valuable articles, Physics, Pneumatics, Præcession of the

Equinoxes, Projectiles, Pumps, Resistance of Fluids, River, Roof, Rope making, Rotation, Seamanship, Signals, Sound, Specific Gravity, Statics, Steam, Steam-Engine, Strength of Materials, Telescope, Tide, Articulating Trumpet, Variation of the Compass, and Water-Works, also Philosophy, in association with Dr. Gleig.

"In the autumn of the year 1797, Professor Robison published an octavo volume, entitled 'Proofs of a Conspiracy, &c.' This volume has been favorably received, and although too hasty a performance for a work of so much consequence, is well entitled, both from its subject and its authenticity, to the serious attention of ever reader.   It arrives at the same remarkable conclusion as the celebrated Memoirs of the Abbe Barruel, illustrating the history of Jacobinism, though the authors were perfectly unconnected with each other, and pursued their inquiries in very different ways.   It has raised (we are sorry for such an appearance) a considerable clamor and enmity against the Professor; though it was written, we are fully convinced, from the best of motives.   We cannot conclude this article without observing that the principles, and honest zeal, which Professor Robison has displayed upon this occasion, are highly creditable to him, and merit the warmest acknowledgements from society in general."

The following is an extract of a letter from one of the most respectable literary characters which Scotland has produced, dated March, 1800. The writer of this letter is now in America. I have not his leave to mention his name.

"Professor Robison's character is so well established among those who know him best, that it would be ridiculous, at Edinburgh, to call in question his veracity or ability. *I had read many of his authorities in the German originals before his book was published;* and the first notice I received of it was, in the preface to Dr. Erskine's sketches of ecclesiastical history, where you will see the honorable testimony that he gives Mr. Robison, and the great expectation that he had from his publication."

The Rev. Dr. Erskine, whose character is generally known, and respected in America, and who is a neighbor to Dr. Robison, in a letter, dated Edinburgh, September 25, 1800, says, "I think highly of Professor Robison's book. Some of the most shocking facts it contains, I knew before its publication, from a periodical account of the church history of the times, by Professor Kœster at Giessen, of which I lent him all the numbers relating to that subject. For three years, that valuable work has been discontinued, whether from the artifices of Illuminati booksellers, to prevent its sale and spread, or from the author's bad health, I know not."

In a subsequent letter, of June 13, 1801, speaking of the forementioned criminations of Dr. Robison's character, which have been circulated in America, the Doctor says, "Had they been sent to Edinburgh, for their PALPABLE FALSEHOOD, they would have been *despised* and *detested*."

In the appendix of the Centurial Sermon of Dr. Dwight, President of Yale College, published Jan. 7, 1801, is an attestation to the character of Professor Robison, taken from a letter of Mr. J. Walker, a respectable inhabitant of Great Britain, to Professor Boëttiger, of Weimar in Germany; published in the Mercury of that city, April, 1800. "It was written in answer to some very sever aspersions on Mr. Robison, by Mr. Boëttiger; and such was the character of the writer, and such the weight of his testimony, that Mr. Boëttiger amply, as well as honorably, retracted his aspersions." Referring to the exalted character he had given of Dr. Robison, he says, "Nor is this the exaggerated praise of a friend; no one who knows Mr. Robison, as I have known him, and he is almost universally known in Britain, will dare to call it in question."*

The character of the Abbe Barruel, so far as it respects his credibility as a witness, I believe has not been impeached. The honest warmth, apparent in every part of his celebrated work, renders it difficult for us to doubt his sincerity, whatever opinion we may form of his judgment. If the fervor of his zeal has hurried him into a rash censure, or an unwarrantable conclusion, does not the same fervor compel us to respect him as a writer, who felt the truth and importance of his subject? Shall we condemn him because he writes with the ardor of the most exquisite feelings? How could he but feel, when he saw the religion and government which he loved, demolished, and the country, above all others dear to him, converted into a field of carnage, and bleeding at every pore, pierced with the daggers of men, who "owed their greatness to their country's ruin?" His attachment to principles not admitted in America, has doubtless weakened the impressions which his testimony ought to have made. While we hear him pleading in support of sentiments in religion, which in our view are absurd; advocating a government, which we consider as tyrannical; and denouncing societies as dangerous, of which we ourselves, perhaps, are innocent members, we naturally connect the absurdity of these sentiments, with the facts adduced in their support. It is an obvious remark, that the

---

* I have further evidence on this subject, but I conceive it needless to introduce it. What is laid before the reader is more than sufficient to establish Dr. Robison's character. It adds no small weight to his opinion; and affords us a degree of assurance, that what he has published upon the subject of Illuminism, is neither visionary nor trifling. The reputation he had acquired in the literary world, forbids us to suppose that he would have added his name to such a publication, unless convinced that the facts he states, and attests, were important and well authenticated.

value of these Memoirs consists, not in the religious or political opinions, but in the important facts, they contain. These appear, generally, to be stated with great accuracy, and with a strict regard to truth; and from these, the author candidly invites us to judge for ourselves. As became an honest man, together with his opinions, he has given us the facts and circumstances upon which that opinion was founded; leaving the reader to correct, if he see cause, his too hasty judgment.

That the Abbe, by making his own sentiments the standard in politics and religion, has censured some persons whom Protestants and republicans would justify, is not to be denied; but has he asserted anything as a fact, without stating carefully the evidence upon which his opinion was founded?

It is obvious that the testimony of these writers is greatly strengthened by its remarkable coincidence. It appears that Dr. Robison's work was published just as the third volume of the Abbe's Memoirs was going to the press, and precisely in those circumstances, which must have prevented either of them from suggesting to the other, either the plan of their proposed publications, or the principal authorities by which they are authenticated. The remarkable difference which appears in these two writers with respect to their methods of arranging, and communicating their thoughts; their very different ideas of religious and political truth; the obscurity which, from the nature of it, attended the subject; the many remote circumstances with which it was connected, and especially the different plans they pursue; Dr. Robison combining, in one paragraph, what his memory compiled from many, while the Abbe, as he declares, "never made a quotation but with the original before him; and when," he says, "I make a translation which may stagger the reader, I subjoin the original, that each may explain and verify the text;" these things taken into view, a greater degree of harmony could not be expected from any two historians relating events of equal magnitude.*

But we have to encounter still more formidable opposition than any which has yet appeared, and that is Professor Ebeling's letter to his correspondent in Massachusetts, and published in the Worchester Gazette, October 9, 1799. This letter appears to have been considered, by some, as containing plenary evidence against the veracity of Dr. Robison, and the credibility of his book. But, had not this letter been read with the same haste and eagerness with which it appears to have been written, certainly so much importance would not have been attached to it.

Upon reading this letter, we naturally recollect an observation made by Professor Renner, one of the witnesses from whom the public received the first disclosure of the Illuminated societies. "There are men;" says he, "who defend the order with great warmth, though they do not declare themselves to belong to it. Such conduct certainly deserves a little animadversion. Either these defenders belong to the order, or they do not; if they do not, can they pretend to defend that which they neither know, nor have any possibility of knowing? If they belong to the order, that

---

* The following testimony, in favor of the authenticity of the works in question, is from a late respectable writer.

"The rise and progress of Jacobinism, which seems to include every species of Infidelity, have been examined with industry, and displayed with correctness, by the Abbe Barruel and Professor Robison. The facts brought forward in support of their assertions, have baffled the ingenuity of Jacobinism itself to disprove. And these facts have clearly shown, that a *conspiracy* was actually formed for the extinction of Christianity, and the abolition of government and social order, by a set of men whose names demand the execration of mankind." Kett, on Prophecy, Lond. edition, 1800, Vol. II, p. 119.

very circumstance renders them unworthy of belief."* The propriety of this remark will impress the reader more forcibly, when he is better acquainted with the arts by which the Illuminees conceal themselves from the public.

The great stress which has been laid upon this letter, and the use which has been made of it, will justify our bestowing on it particular attention.

It may be of some importance to recollect, that Mr. Ebeling has acknowledged that it was written in haste, and was, consequently, inaccurate. It was unfortunate that this information was not communicated, as usual, at the close of the letter, where it might have been useful to guard us against placing too much dependence on a hasty and inaccurate performance; but it was given in a subsequent letter, after being informed that the previous one had been made public. Though this apology came too late for us, it may be useful to the Professor, and afford him a retreat, should some of his many confident declarations, hereafter appear to be founded in error.

Mr. Ebeling considers Dr. Robison's misrepresentations, as the result of wicked intention; speaks of him as "an *English hired, ministerial writer;*" and tells us, "his book is certainly a party work, and not without a *political design.*" In another part of the same letter he ascribes Robison's misrepresentations to his "*great ignorance of men, manners, and history,* and of *German characters, and language* in particular." Perhaps Mr. Ebeling can reconcile these two contradictory causes of the same effect. The talk is beyond my ability. From these very different representations, I can obtain no idea but this absurd one, that Dr. Robison was hired by the British ministry, to give such a wrong view of things as would serve their political purposes; that he

* Barruel's Memoirs, Vol. IV, p. 149.

undertook the task, and by the luckiest mistake stumbled upon that very spot at which he was aiming, and which, had it not been for his gross ignorance of men, manners, and history, of German characters, and language, he probably never would have attained. Let this form a new item among the advantages of ignorance.

But we have more important remarks to make upon this celebrated letter. Mr. Ebeling speaks of the existence of Illuminism in Germany, as a matter of public notoriety; but, to preserve the impression of its harmless nature, he says of the Illuminees, "their design was undoubtedly to prevent political and religious oppression;" and with a particular reference to Weishaupt, the grand projector of Illuminism, further adds, "he was, as I suppose commonly Roman Catholics are, when they see the errors of superstition, and know nothing of the Protestant faith, or true religion, *at a loss what to substitute.*" Weishaupt then, it is confessed, wished to destroy the best religion he was acquainted with. He considered popery as the religion of the Bible, and this was hateful superstition. It appears, therefore, from this statement of his Apologist, that he would have spared no religion, for in his view there was no substitute for popery. The reader will observe, that Weishaupt was a Professor in an University, and distinguished for his literary acquirements; that he had framed many new systems of Christianity to deceive his adepts; that Germany abounded with Protestants of every denomination, but still there was no religion to his taste, no substitute for popery.

Mr. Ebeling also acknowledges that Weishaupt, "in his younger life, was guilty of *great deviations from pure morality,*" but in the same paragraph in which he gives us this view of his moral character, and in the same paragraph in which he acknowledges, that Weishaupt could find no religion in all Germany, nor in the Bible, better than popery, which he hated, and was endeavoring to overturn; Mr. Ebeling displays his invincible charity by adding, "but I am not convinced that he (Weishaupt) *was every in theory, or PRACTICE, an enemy to religion!!*" Lest the reader should not extend that charity to Mr. Ebeling, of which he himself is so liberal, it may be necessary here to remind him, that the Professor wrote in haste. In the confusion of his thoughts he must have lost the impression which Weishaupt's character had formerly made upon his mind, and in the hurry of the moment, he marked the *infidel and the debauchee, for a Christian;* for nothing less he be who never was, "either in theory or practice, an enemy to religion."

One great disadvantage, indeed, results from this exuberance of the Professor's hasty charity, for who can assure us, that he has not equally mistaken the many other characters, he introduces into his letter? This consideration must diminish that fund of correct information, which some imagine they possess in this long epistle, and leave us room to doubt, at least, whether Dr. Robison *was so very ignorant* of men and manners as he is represented.

But will not this letter assist us in attaining something beyond probabilities and conjecture? Mr. Ebeling has said much to discredit the other authorities to which Dr. Robison occasionally recurs for proof; but I find nothing to weaken the evidence resulting from the testimony of the four very respectable witnesses, given under oath, respecting the practices of the Illuminees; nor, as far as I am able to ascertain, does he express a doubt respecting the writings, letters, and documents, found in the hands of the Society on the search made in consequence of the testimony abovementioned. Here we have the code of the Society, their private correspondence, and their own remarks upon the nature and design of the institution; these are admitted to be genuine; and on these, as their proper basis, Robison and Barruel raise their superstructure. Have we not here a clue, which will lead us out of this labyrinth of discordant opinions? Let us examine carefully, the ground on which we stand.

It is agreed, that a Society of Illuminees existed in Germany, instituted by Weishaupt, about the year 1776. It is agreed, that the papers found in the possession of Counselor Zwack, in 1786, and those found in the Castle of Sanderdorf, in 1787, on search made by order of his Highness the Elector of Bavaria, are authentic documents, drawn up by the Illuminees, expressing the plan and object of the order. It is agreed, that the object of this institution is the overthrow of all religion, and all government. No; — this, though strangely asserted by Messrs. Robison and Barruel, Mr. Ebeling denies. To determine on which side the truth lies, we must appeal to the papers which are admitted to be authentic, and from them judge for ourselves what were the real views of the Illuminees. By attacking every other witness in the cause, Mr. Ebeling, by his silence, concerning the papers, has implicitly acknowledged their truth and validity.

The reader is here reminded, that the question to be determined is not, whether Illuminism had an existence; this is admitted: Nor whether it existed as an organized body, possessing its code of laws, and definite mode of operation; for Mr. Ebeling himself informs us, that the Illuminees were instituted, or formed into a body, about 1776. Nor is it a question whether this order of men had anything in view beyond their own amusement, for the same advocate of their cause observes, "that their design undoubtedly was, to prevent political and religious oppression." But the important question to be determined is, whether this combination of men had not a higher object? Whether their ultimate aim was not the subversion of every social, moral, and religious obligation? Taking this for our object, it will be needless to introduce into this work that part of the evidence above referred to, which relates particularly to the subversion of the Romish hierarchy and despotism, or political and religious oppression; for all acknowledge that these were aimed at by the conspiracy. Our present concern is, with that part only of these writings which relates to the principal question, and is calculated to prove, that the Illuminees were opposed to the fundamental principals of all religion, and social order.

The Abbe Barruel's Memoirs comprehend a larger period of time than Dr. Robison's work; his arrangements are more systematical, and he traces the evil to its source; his method, without, however, being confined to it, will be principally followed.

The Abbe Barruel's plan includes,

First. The *Anti-Christian Conspiracy,* or that of the Sophisters of impiety against Christianity, under every form and denominations.

Secondly. The *Anti-Monarchical Conspiracy.* This part will be omitted in the following work, as unconnected with the question in view, and because it is involved in the

Third, or *Anti-Social Conspiracy,* in which the sophisters of impiety, coalesce with the sophisters of Anarchy against every religion, and every government, under the denomination of *Illuminees;* and, *these* again unite themselves with the occult Lodges of Free Masons, and thus form the club of the *Jacobins* at Paris, who are the real directors of the French Revolution. This *third part* embraces the subject of the Conspiracy of which Dr. Robison treats; and is more particularly interesting in our present inquiry.

The *evidence* adduced in proof of the *Anti-Christian Conspiracy,* are the writings of the Conspirators themselves; especially the Edition of Voltaire's Works, by Beaumarchis.

These Works, it appears, were published when the sentiments they contain, were no longer considered as infamous in France.*

The Author of these Memoirs declares it to be the important and friendly design of his undertaking, to warn governments and mankind of their danger, by proving to them, that the French Revolution, in all the circumstance of horror which attended it, was the natural result of the principals from which it proceeded; and that *similar principals will produce similar effects.* Lest any, confiding in their leagues of amity with France, and her professions of friendship, should imagine the warning needless with respect to themselves, he again sounds the alarm.   Let America hear!

"When the phantom of peace shall seam to terminate the present war, between the Jacobins and the combined powers, it certainly will be the interest of all governments to ascertain how far such a peace can be relied on.   At that period, more than any other, will it be necessary to study the secret history of that sect; at that period we must remember, that it is not in the field of Mars that the war against sects is the most dangerous; that is a war of plots and conspiracies, and against them public treaties can never avail."†

---

* The proofs of the Anti-Social Conspiracy will be noticed in connection with that part of the subject to which they relate. The reader will not expect to find, in this work, the particular references of the larger work, transcribed; except where some authority, not before mentioned, is introduced. This would be needless, as the few, who would wish to recur to the original authorities, may find every necessary reference in the translation of Barruel's Memoirs, printed at Hartford, by Hudson and Goodwin, 1799; and in the fourth Edition of Robison's Proofs, &c. printed at New York, by George Forman, in 1799; which are the Editions made use of in forming this abstract.

† Preliminary Discourse, Barruel's Memoirs, Vol. I.

Chapter I.

The Actors, Existence, Object, and Secret of the Conspiracy

P H E N O M E N A of the most astonishing nature have, within a few years past, arrested the attention of mankind. Manners, and the state of society, have undergone a revolution which has appeared to extinguish, in many, every natural affection, and to transform the most civilized and polished, into the most ferocious of men. The best established principles of natural and revealed religion, and the very foundations of moral and social duty, obligations never before controverted, have been attacked by an host of enemies. A flood on infidelity has deluged the greater part of the Christianized world, threatening to sweep away every vestige of Christianity. And may it not be said, almost without a metaphor, that by an horrid Anti-Christian regeneration, a nation of Atheists have been born in a day?

These are plain facts; and they demand the most serious attention of mankind. It is not by framing fanciful theories, but by carefully tracing effects to their causes, that we acquire useful knowledge and experience. Some adequate cause, there must have been, of this mighty mischief. Whence shall we date its origin? To what shall we ascribe its rise and progress? In answer to these queries we presume to say, that however accessory other causes may have been, the principal cause is to be found in the following historical abstract.

About the middle of the last century there appear three men, leagued in the most inveterate hatred against Christianity, VOLTAIRE the Chief, D'ALEMBART, distinguished for his subtilty, and FREDERIC II. King of Prussia; to which number was afterwards added DIDEROT, whom, probably on account of his frantic impiety, the historian characterizes, the *forlorn hope.*

The necessary brevity of this work will not permit us to descend to a particular view of their several characters, yet the first of these conspirators is so distinguished in this work, and in the literary world, as to justify a more particular attention.

Voltaire, the son of an ancient notary of the Chatelet, was born at Paris, February 20, 1694. His original name was Mary Francis Arouet, which, through vanity, he changed to Voltaire, as more sonorous, and more comfortable to the reputation at which he aimed. He was eminently distinguished for his abilities, and for his thirst of dominion over the literary world. His talents, however, were more brilliant than solid, less fitted for deep investigation, but eminently calculated to amuse and captivate. He possessed all those passions which render abilities dangerous; and, unhappily, his appeared to be all early devoted to the overthrow of religion. While a student, he received the following prophetic rebuke from his Professor: "Unfortunate young man, you will one day come to be the standard-bearer of infidelity."*

After leaving the College he associated with men of abandoned morals; and having given offence to the French government by some satirical essays, he sought asylum in

---

* Life of Voltaire, Edit. of Kell.

PROOF OF THE ILLUMINATI

England. There he first conceived the design of over-throwing religion, by *blending Philosophy with Impiety.* Condorcet, his adept, his confident, his historian, and panegyrist, asserts in positive terms, *"There it was that Voltaire swore to dedicate his life to the accomplishment of that project; and he has kept his word."**

On his return to Paris, about the year 1730, he became so open in his designs, and so sanguine in his hopes, that Mr. Herault, the lieutenant of Police, remarked to him, *"You may do or write what you please, you will never be able to destroy the Christian religion."* Voltaire, without hesitation, answered, *"That is what we shall see."*†

While he yet flattered himself with the hopes of enjoy-ing, alone, the whole glory of destroying the Christian religion, (though he soon found that associates would be necessary,) *"I am weary"* he would say, *"of hearing people repeat, that twelve men have been sufficient to establish Christianity, and I will prove that one may suffice to over-throw it."*‡

Frederic also, dignified among the sophisters, with the title of "the Solomon of the North," and by the historian with the epithet of "The Great," claims, even in this brief sketch, a more particular notice. To express his contrary, and almost irreconcilable qualities, we find him painted a double man, exhibiting two distinct and opposite charac-ters. In one view of him, we see the hero, and the father of his people, giving life to agriculture and commerce; in another, the sophister, the philosophical pedant, the con-spirator against Christianity. The contradictions in his character are transcribed in his letters; at one time, extol-

---

* Ibid.
† Ibid.
‡ Ibid.

ling, in glowing terms, the morality of the gospel; and at
another, asserting that *"Christianity yields none but poisonous weeds."*

There can be no doubt, however, that Frederic united
cordially, as he did early, with the enemies of religion. Even
at that early age, when he was only Prince-Royal, in his
correspondence with Voltaire, he had adopted the style of
the modern Philosopher; for he thus writes, "To speak with
my usual freedom, I must naturally own, that whatever
regards the *God made man,* displeases me in the mouth of a
Philosopher, who should be above popular error. We may
speak of fables, but merely as fables; and a profound silence,
in my opinion, should be kept, concerning those fables of
the Christians, sanctified by time and the credulity of the
absurd and stupid."[*]

But what did this boasted wisdom avail? While soaring,
in imagination, far above their fellow mortals, we see them
in the same situation in which every person will find
himself, who relinquishes the guiding light of Revelation,
wandering in the wilderness without a path, and without a
compass. "Is there a God such as he is said to be? A soul
such as is imagined? Is there anything to be hoped for after
this life?" These questions, the *comfortable* fruits of infidelity, were proposed by Voltaire to D'Alembert; to which he
answers, with the same *admirable* philosophic wisdom, that

---

[*] As Frederic is another of Mr. Ebeling's Christians, who, he inti-
mates, died in the hope of a better life, I beg leave to introduce a short
sketch of his character, drawn by a skilful, and apparently, impartial
pen. "Most unjustly (says the writer) is he styled *great;* a philosophical
monarch, the most despotic, perhaps, who ever existed, but who has
contributed more to the dissolution of society, by corrupting the
principals and morals of all within the sphere of his influence, than any
individual of his time." See Appendix to Vol. 6, of Anti-Jacobin Review,
p. 565.

"*No*, in metaphysics, appeared to him not much wiser than *yes*; and that *non liquet* (it is not clear) was generally the only rational answer."* Who would not give up the Bible for the honor and comfort of being so nobly and philosophically bewildered?

Sensible that the individual infidelity of these persons did not constitute a conspiracy against Christianity, without a union and correspondence in the attack, the historian has furnished us with the proofs of such a confederacy, in which their efforts, and those of their adepts, appear combined and steadily pointed to the accomplishment of their grand object. To this object they directed and stimulated each other by a watchword, strikingly expressive of their rancorous enmity to the Savior, *ecrasez l'infamè! crush the wretch.* But could this mean Christ, and that adorable religion preached by him and his apostles? What other interpretation can we annex to the phrase in the mouth of a man, who, in his intrigues against "the wretch," exclaims, "Could not five or six men of parts, and who rightly understood each other, succeed, after the examples of *twelve scoundrels,* who have already succeeded?" And who thus writes to D'Alembert, "Both you and Demilaville must be well pleased, to see the contempt into which 'the wretch' is fallen among the better sort of people throughout Europe. They were all we wished for, or that were necessary. We never pretended to enlighten the house maids, and shoe makers; we leave them to the apostles."†

In the true style of conspirators, they had also their enigmatical language, and secret appropriate names. The general term for the conspirators was *Cacouac;* they say one is a good Cacouac, when he can be perfectly depended on.

---

* Barruel's Memoirs, Vol. I. Chap. 1.

† Barruel's Memoirs, Vol. I. Chap. 2.

In their correspondence, Frederic is called Duluc; Voltaire, Raton; D'Alembert, Protagoras and Bertrand; Diderot, Plato or Tamplot. Secrecy appears to have been considered by them as essential to their success. Their Chief would therefore often remind them that in the war they waged, "they were to act as conspirators, and not as zealots. Strike," he would say, "hurl the Javelin, but hide your hand."

Voltaire had long before vented his rage against Christianity, and been the officious defender of every impious publication; but, about 1752, when he returned from Berlin, the conspiracy assumed a regular form, and he, by his age, reputation, and genius, naturally became the chief.*

* Barruel's Memoirs, Vol. I. Chap. 3.

Chapter II.

The Means of the Conspirators

ESTABLISHED in the general process of under-mining the Christian Edifice, and thus obliging it to fall of itself, as one powerful means of effecting this end, an Encyclopedia was projected by D'Alembert, and announced to the world, as a complete treasure of all human arts and sciences, but which, in reality, was designed to be the emporium of all the sophisms and calumnies which had ever been invented against religion. This poison, however, was to be conveyed in the most secret and unsuspicious manner, and it was declared, that all the religious articles should be complied by learned and orthodox divines. Particular care was taken in the compilation of the first volume, not to alarm the friends of religion; reserving a clearer expression of their sentiments for succeeding volumes.

Among the many artful means adopted to communicate the secret infection, one was, to insinuate error and infidelity, not where it would have been expected, but into those articles deemed least susceptible of them; such as History, Natural Philosophy, and Chemistry.*

---

* Mr. Paley, in his System of Moral Philosophy, has noticed, and very justly described, the subtle arts of modern impiety. "Infidelity is now served up in every shape that is likely to allure, surprise, or beguile the

35

Another was that of reference, by which, after being presented with some religious truths, the reader is invited to seek further information in articles of a different cast. Sometimes the reference would direct to an epigram, or sarcasm. After having treated a religious subject with all possible respect, it would be simply added, See the article *Prejudice,* or *Superstition,* or *Fanaticism.**

The following may serve as a specimen of the artful use of references, in this work, for undermining religious truth. Under the article GOD, you find sound sentiments, together with a direct and complete proof of his existence. From this the reader is referred to the article *Demonstration.* There all direct demonstrations of the existence of God disappear; and we are told, that a single insect more forcibly proves the being of a God, than any other arguments whatever. But the render is still referred to the article *Corruption.* There it is asserted, that daily experiments seem to prove, that "Corruption may produce animated bodies." The reader is thus left to infer, if he pleases, that the strongest proof of the existence of a God is contradicted by daily experiments.

Notwithstanding all this art and concealment, the work met with great opposition, and was for a time suspended. At length, however, it was completed, and all the adepts were loud in its praises. The learned were duped. The work sold. Various editions were published, and under the pretense of correcting, each succeeding edition was more highly charged with infidelity.†

The Encyclopedia having prepared the way, was suc-

---

imagination; in a fable, a tale, a novel, a poem, in interspersed and broken hints; remote and oblique surmises; in books of travels, of philosophy, of natural history; in a word, in any form rather than that of a professed and regular disquisition." Paley, Boston Edit. 1795, p. 302.

* Barruel's Memoirs, Vol. I. Chap. 4.

† Barruel's Memoirs, Vol. I. Chap. 4. Note.

ceeded by an attempt to overturn the religious orders. This ended in the suppression of many of them, and in the expulsion of the Jesuits, in 1764. The artful movements, by which this was effected, are not sufficiently interesting to claim a particular detail. Some, who appear to have been friendly to the Romish establishment, but not sufficiently considering the connection between a church and its clergy, were drawn by these sophisters to countenance, and even promote the suppression of the religious orders; and we see these conspirators ridiculing, in secret, the simplicity of their dupes.*

Mankind were extremely deceived by the insincere professions of the conspirators. Nothing, perhaps, contributed more to their success than their pretensions to *toleration, reason,* and *humanity.* But notwithstanding these high sounding words, their secret correspondence betrays the same spirit which has since been exhibited in the revolution. Was it *humanity* which dictated to Voltaire his wish, "to see every Jesuit at the bottom of the ocean, with a Jansenist at his neck?" He was much engaged to deprive the ecclesiastical princes of their possessions, and the clergy of their means of support; and exerted his influence, with Frederic, and the Duke of Praslin in particular, for this end. Writing to Count Argental upon this subject, he says, "Had I but an hundred thousand men, I well know what I would do with them." Would he then preach tolerance and humanity? We may judge from his own expressions what his views were. "It is noble," he writes to Frederic, "to scoff at these Harlequin Bull-givers. I like to cover them with ridicule, *but I had rather plunder them.*"†

Protestants will perhaps consider the suppression of

---

* Barruel's Memoirs, Vol. I. Chap. 5, 6.
† Barruel's Memoirs, Vol. I. Chap. 10.

these orders as having no connection with the interests of religion; but they were the great props of this cause as it existed in France; were active in withstanding the progress of infidelity, and their overthrow was undoubtedly, as it was viewed by those conspirators, of great importance to the completion of their ultimate design; the establishment of universal infidelity.

Wearied with the opposition he met with in France, and the constant constraint to which he was subjected, Voltaire projected the establishment of a colony of Philosophers, at Cleves, under the jurisdiction of Frederic, who might there, as he expresses his views, "freely and boldly speak the truth, without fear of ministers, priests, or parliaments." But this, though a favorite object with the projector, proved abortive. The conspirators were too much captivated with the pleasures of Paris, and the applause they found in the circles of their admirers, to be fond of such a retirement; and least of all, was it eligible, in company with Voltaire, whose more splendid genius would eclipse his satellites.*

But a more important attempt, met with different success. The highest literary honor in France was a seat in the French Academy. This institution, designed to be both a stimulus, and a reward to literary merit, had enjoyed the special favor and protection of the kings of France; and none but men of eminence in some branch of literature, and who were viewed as friendly to morals and religion, had been admitted as members. The artful D'Alembert concealed his infidelity until he had gained a seat. Voltaire was for a long time unable to gain admission, and at length only succeeded by means of high protections, and that low hypocrisy which he recommended to his disciples.

The conspirators justly estimated the advantages which

---

* Barruel's Memoirs, Vol. I. Chap. 7.

would result to their grand object, by removing the dis-
qualifying bar of infidelity, and annexing to philosophism
the respectability and influence of such an institution.
Upon Voltaire and D'Alembert lay the task, of converting
these dignified seats of science into the haunts of Atheism.
We may judge of their success, from the following anecdote.
Mr. Beauzet, a member of the academy, respectable for his
piety, when asked how he could ever have been associated
with such notorious unbelievers?   "The very same question," said he, "I put to D'Alembert. At one of the sittings,
seeing that *I was nearly the only person who believed in God,*
I asked him, how he possibly could have thought of me for a
member, when he knew that my sentiments and opinions
differed so widely from those of his brethren? D'Alembert,
without hesitation, answered, 'We were in want of a skillful
grammarian, and among our party, not one had made
himself a reputation in that line.'"   It is almost needless to
remark, that the rewards of literary merit were henceforth
transferred to the advocates of impiety, while reproach and
infamy were profusely cast upon those who espoused the
cause of truth.*

Their success in securing the Academy to themselves,
prepared the way for that variety of Anti-Christian writings,
which of late have been so widely disseminated, and which
have been pointed against religion. Astonishing efforts were
made to weaken the evidences of the Christian history. The
surface of the earth underwent a new survey, and its bowels
were explored, not to promote the interests of literature,
which was the ostensible object, not to obtain the pious
pleasure which the good man feels in contemplating the
works of the Creator; but,

---

* Barruel's Memoirs, Vol. I. Chap. 8.

———— "Some drill and bore
The solid earth, and from the strata there
Extract a register, by which we learn
That he who made it and reveal'd its date
To Moses, was mistaken in its age."

Yet then, as now, they who were alarmed by these Anti-Christian theories, and gave warning of the danger, were held up to the public as weakly timid, "For what," it was impudently asked, "have philosophical treatises to do with religion?"

But while Voltaire saw the expediency, of what he calls, *"some serious work,"* some publication which should have the semblance of reason and philosophy, the weapon on which he principally depended, was ridicule. Deists have long found this their best mode of attack; but the genius of Voltaire was peculiarly fruitful in anecdotes, jests, and sarcasms. "I only ask," he writes to D'Alembert, "five or six witticisms a day, that would suffice. It (meaning 'the wretch') would not get the better of them. Laugh Democritus, make me laugh, and the sages shall carry the day."

But not content with engrossing literary honors, the conspirators condescended, at length, to enlighten those whom they had contemptuously called the house maids and shoe makers. Writings, in every form and shape, calculated to excite licentious desires, to deprave the moral taste, to communicate the infection of infidelity, and exhibit religion in a ridiculous view, were crowded upon the public.

Upon the commencement of the revolution, it appeared, by the confession of Le Roy, who had been their secretary, that a society, which had existed for a considerable time, holding their meetings at the Hotel de Holbach, at Paris, under the name of Economists, was composed of these conspirators and their principal adepts; and who, while professedly engaged in promoting economy, agriculture, and the useful arts, were more actively promoting the cause of infidelity. A multitude of writers were employed to prepare suitable publications. These, previous to their going to the press, were subjected to the inspection of the society, whose care it was to charge them with a due proportion of the poisonous leaven they were designed to disseminate. To add respectability to these writings, and conceal the author, the society appointed under what title they should be published. For instance, "*Christianity Unveiled*," was attributed to Boulanger, after his death, but was the work of Demilaville.

Elegant editions of these works were first printed to defray the expense, and then an immense number on the poorest paper. These latter, were distributed in bales, free of cost, or at a very low price, to hawkers and peddlers, who would disperse them through the country, and lest any should escape the infection, clubs were formed, and persons hired to read them to such as were unable to read.

Mr. Bertin, one of the French ministry, declares, that in his excursions into the country, he found the peddlers loaded with the writings of Voltaire, Diderot, and other philosophists; and that, questioning them how the country people could find money for such dear works, their constant answer was, "We have them at a much cheaper rate than *Prayer Books;* we may sell them at ten sols (5 *d.*) a volume, and have a pretty profit into the bargain;" and many of them owned that these books cost them nothing.

But the question in which we are principally interested is, whether it was the design of these numerous publications to affect anything more than that deformed excrescence of Christianity, popery? If it has not been made evident that these writings were aimed, not at the abuses of Christianity, but at Christianity itself, a view of the leading sentiments in these publications, must remove every doubt.

Freret tells us expressly, that, "The God of the Jews, and of the Christians, is but a phantom and a chimera;" and that, "all ideas of justice and injustice, of virtue and vice, are arbitrary, and dependent on custom."

The author of *"Good Sense,"* a work which D'Alembert wished to see abridged, that it might be sold for *five pence* to the poor and ignorant, teaches, "That the wonders of nature, so far from bespeaking a God, are but the necessary effects of matter, prodigiously diversified, and that the soul is a chimera."

The author of the *"Doubts"* tells mankind, "That they cannot know whether a God really exists, or whether there exists the smallest difference between virtue and vice."

Helvetius informs the fair sex, "That modesty is only an invention of refined voluptuousness." He teaches children, "That the commandment of loving their parents, is more the work of education than nature;" and the married couple, "That the law which condemns to live together, becomes barbarous and cruel on the day they cease to love each other."

The author of *"Christianity Unveiled,"* has this remark, "The Bible says, the fear of the Lord is the beginning of wisdom. I think it rather the beginning of folly."

But I shall only add to this detail, *John Meslier's last will,* in which he is represented "on his death bed, imploring forgiveness of his God for having taught Christianity;" a work, of which Voltaire urges D'Alembert to print and distribute four or five thousand copies; complaining "that there were not so many in all Paris, as he himself had distributed throughout the mountains of Switzerland."*

The conspirators appear to have been aware of the importance of youth, and the advantage to be derived to

* Barruel's Memoirs, Vol. I. Chap. 9, 17; and Note.

their cause, by an early impression on the young mind. D'Alembert, less qualified to promote the views of the conspirators by his pen, attended more particularly to providing instructors. Care was taken that he should receive early notice of vacant professorships in colleges, and of vacant schools, that they might be filled agreeably to their wishes. It will be readily conceived that pupils of rank, wealth, and talents, would engage special attention. D'Alembert was the open protector of all such, who visited Paris. The extensive correspondence of Voltaire, and the eclat of his genius, gave a vast opportunity of infecting youth, even in foreign courts.

At that time the court of Parma was seeking men worthy to preside over the education of the young infant. The account which Voltaire gave of the result of that business, will abundantly explain the views of the conspirators in this point. Writing to D'Alembert, he says, "It appears to me that the Parmesan child will be well surrounded. He will have a Condilhac and a de Leire. *If with all that he is a bigot, grace must be powerful indeed.*"*

Among the innumerable attempts of these ever plotting philosophists, the following curious instance of zeal is related of Diderot and D'Alembert. They frequently met in the coffee houses at Paris, to discuss religious questions, before the idle Parisians. In these disputes Diderot would appear in his proper character of an infidel, D'Alembert assuming that of an advocate for religion; and apparently espousing its cause with great warmth, until driven by the victorious infidel from every ground of defense, he would retreat, to appearance chagrined, and regretting that his religion afforded no better arguments for its defense. The impression which such a scene must leave upon the minds

* Barruel's Memoirs, Vol. I. Chap 11.

of those present, who were ignorant of the deception, need not be told.*

Their desire to *"crush the wretch,"* suggested also to these conspirators the idea of rebuilding the temple at Jerusalem, with a view of defeating the predictions of Christ, and the prophet Daniel. This had been long since attempted by Julian the apostate, with the same design, when flames and balls of fire bursting from the foundations, and repeatedly destroying the workmen, compelled him to desist from his purpose.† This rendered D'Alembert and Voltaire more desirous of depriving Scripture prophecy of such a glorious attestation to its truth. With this view, application was made both to Frederic and the Empress of Russia, to engage them to use their influence with the Turkish powers to whom jurisdiction Jerusalem pertained, to promote the design; but the fear of losing many wealthy Jews, whom they found profitable subjects, and who, in that case, would have repaired to their new temple, prevented the attempt.‡

To reconcile many things, of a very different aspect in the conduct and writings of these men, with the purposes here attributed to them, it is necessary the reader should be informed, that all these designs were industriously concealed under a covert of hypocrisy. Voltaire had completely convinced them of the utility of his favorite maxim, "strike, but hide your hand." Their real views were obvious, indeed, to the more discerning, but many were duped by what

---

* Ibid.

† This miracle is recorded by many witnesses, and more particularly by Ammianus Marcellinus, a pagan author, and friend of Julian. The truth of this miracle is denied, indeed, by Basnage; but its authenticity appears to be fully established in a learned dissertation upon the subject, by Dr. Warburton, in which the objections of Basnage are particularly examined, and refuted.

‡ Barruel's Memoirs, Vol. I. Chap 11.

D'Alembert calls, *"his vows to religion,"* and Voltaire boasts much of the success of his master stroke of policy, "in erecting a church, and constantly receiving communion."*

---

* Ibid.

Chapter III.

Progress of the Conspiracy; the Triumph, and Death of the Chiefs

P OWERFUL must have been the operation of such abilities, subtlety, and zeal. With Frederic of Prussia, Voltaire classes, in the number of his adepts, Joseph II, emperor of Germany, Catherine II, empress of Russia, Christiern VII, king of Denmark, Gustavus III, king of Sweden, Ulrica, queen of Sweden, and Poniatowski, king of Poland.

Among the princes and princesses, Frederic, landgrave of Hesse Cassel, the Duke of Brunswick, Lois Eugene, duke of Wirtemberg, and Lois, prince of Wirtemberg, Charles Theodora, elector palatine, the princess Anhault Zerbst, and Wilhelmina, margravine of Barieth, are also ranked with the initiated.*

A great part of the ministry, the nobles, and higher class of citizens in France, and, (excepting the clergy, who for the

---

* That these personages were in the habits of friendly correspondence with Voltaire, were captivated with his abilities, and charmed with the pleasing sounds of reason and philosophy, is undoubted; but that they wished the destruction of religion, separate from the abuses of popery, does not appear, unless from the boastings of the conspirators. Frederic, Christiern of Denmark, the landgrave of Hesse, Wilhelmina of Barieth, if no more, are however to be excepted from this remark. Barruel's Memoirs, Vol. I. Chap. 12 and 13.

most part remained firm in the cause of religion) the literati, not of France only, but of Europe in general, appear to have been ensnared with this fascinating philosophy. Nor was in confined to men of science. Voltaire boasts, "That there was not a Christian to be found from Geneva to Bern; that Germany gave him great hopes; Russia still greater, and that in Spain as well as Italy a great revolution was operating in ideas."

It was these prospects of success, probably, which led him to utter that most blasphemous prediction, *"That in twenty years more, God will be in a pretty plight."**

The amazing influence of these writings is to be found, not in their superior excellence of any kind, but in the magic sounds of reason and philosophy. The historian justly remarks, that had Voltaire and D'Alembert called themselves enemies of Christianity, they would have been the execration of Europe. But while only calling themselves philosophers, they are mistaken for such. Voltaire, by his superior abilities, had gained such ascendancy in the literary world, that whatever he was pleased to call philosophy, became current with all whose abject minds depended on the opinions of others; and Voltaire was very liberal in applying the term to whatever was impious. He boasts of many philosophers in Paris *behind the counter.*† What! shall

---

* Barruel's Memoirs, Vol. I. Chap. 18.

† If Voltaire's judgement was not entirely perverted by his enmity to religion, whenever he reflected upon his curious herd of philosophers, he must have been diverted with the ridiculous idea. A man may, indeed, be ignorant of philosophy, and the liberal arts, and yet be highly respectable, while his professional employment does not render an acquaintance with these subjects necessary. But for such a man to claim the title of philosopher, and to claim it simply upon the foundation of his ridiculing that holy religion as absurd, which a Newton, a Locke, an Addison, a Jones, and some of the greatest men of every age have believed and defended; if anything is a proper object of disgust, it is

every wanton coquette; shall every husband or wife who scoffs at conjugal fidelity; shall every son who denies the authority of a parent; the courtier destitute of morals, and the man who is a slave to his passions; shall these be styled philosophers?*

As a useful comment on the foregoing exhibition of successful wickedness, we are now called to witness the closing scene of the tragic actors.

I beg leave here to remark for myself, that I feel a sensible concern in republishing this scene, not to offend against the reverence which becomes an imperfect creature, in tracing the awful footsteps of JEHOVAH; nor would I willingly become accessory in promoting an undue use of providential dispensations. Ever odious to me is the practice of supporting our particular opinions and party distinctions, by a bold and unwarranted application of God's high and mysterious providence; and far am I from wishing to encourage this sentiment, that men will receive, in this world, according to their works; but, that many events in providence may be, and ought to be considered, as confirmations of revealed truth, and the *God* is sometimes *to be known by the judgments which he executes,* none, I presume, who admit the truth of revelation, will deny.

The conspiracy exhibited an instance unparalleled in the history of man. In Voltaire, we behold, not simply an unbeliever, a man hurried into sinful indulgences by the impulse of violent appetites, but the bold, active, determined enemy of God and religion, deliberately devoting his uncommon abilities to the dishonor of the giver, and the

---

such a wretched compound of pride and ignorance. Of such philosophers it is emphatically true, *"That professing themselves to be wise, they become fools."*

* Barruel's Memoirs, Vol. I. Chap. 19.

seduction of his fellow creatures from their allegiance to their Maker. Did not this mischief, this communicated poison seem to require a powerful antidote? And may we not image *compassion* as imploring the Father of his creatures, to afford some extraordinary means for delivering the minds of men from the violence they had suffered, by the perversion of such uncommon talents?

Such is the tendency of the following interesting scene. Let the world draw near and receive instruction! Let mankind duly estimate the boasted powers of human reasons, and the fruits of that philosophy, which proudly rejects the offered comforts of the gospel!

The French government has testified their disapprobation of Voltaire's writings, by prohibiting his visiting Paris. His numerous partisans, at length, succeed in procuring a suspension of this sentence; and their chief, now in the eighty-fourth year of his age, is once more permitted to make his appearance at the capital. The academies and theaters confer on him their richest honors; and the adepts, in his triumph, celebrate their own. So sensibly did he enjoy this adulation, that he exclaimed, *"You then wish to make me expire with glory."* But whatever was their design, the will of Providence was very different from this; for, in the midst of his triumphs, he was seized with a violent hemorrhage,* and his conscience was alarmed with the more insupportable terrors of the Almighty. In the first part of his sickness, he applied to a Romish priest, and gave in a declaration of his repentance; but the sophisters interfered, and prevented its being completed according to the ritual of that church. Remorse and rage filled the remainder of his wretched days; now supplicating, and now blaspheming that Savior whom he had sworn *to crush;* and

---

* A violent flux of blood.

in plaintive accents he would cry out, "Oh Christ! Oh Jesus Christ!" And then complain that he was abandoned by God and man. The hand which had traced the sentence of an impious, revelling king, seemed to trace before his eyes, *"Crush then, do crush the wretch."*

"Begone," he would exclaim to the conspirators who approached him, *"It is you who have brought me to my present state, and what a wretched glory have you procured me!"* his physicians and attendants were compelled, by the horrors of the scene, to retire. Mr. Tronchin, his principal physician, declared, that *"the furies of Arestes could give but faint idea of those of Voltaire."*

Thus died, on the 30th of May, 1778, three months after his first seizure, worn out by his own fury, rather than by disease and the decay of years, the most malignant conspirator against Christianity that had lived since the time of the apostles.*

After the death of Voltaire, D'Alembert conducted the affairs of the conspiracy, of which he was the proclaimed chief. He died November, 1783, five years after his patron; and from what can be collected, it appears, that he derived no better comforts from his boasted philosophy. Condorcet undertook to render him inaccessible to all who would willingly declare the truth, and in particular, violently excluded the Rector of St. Germain's, who presented himself in the quality of a pastor; yet when first relating the circumstance of his death, he hesitated not to add, *"Had I not*

---

* The above facts are grounded on judicial minutes, deposited at Paris, in the hands on Mons. Momet, Notary Public, and on the testimony of the celebrated Mr. Tronchin. This testimony is confirmed by a letter from M. De Luc, sent to Abbe Barruel, after the appearance of the first volume of these Memoirs, and which may be seen in the appendix to the third volume.

been there he would have flinched also."* The adept, Grim, writing an account of his death to Frederic, says, "That sickness had greatly weakened D'Alembert's mind in his last moments."

Diderot in his last sickness, upon being faithfully admonished of his danger by a young man who attended him, melted into tears; applied to a clergyman, Mr. De Tersac, and was preparing a recantation of his errors, when his situation was discovered by the sophisters. With much difficulty they persuaded him that a country air would relieve him. The wretches concealed his departure, and supported him with these delusive hopes, when they knew his last hour was fast approaching. They watched him till they had seen him expire, and then represented that he died in all his atheism, without any signs of remorse.

Frederic alone, succeeded in persuading himself, that death was an everlasting sleep.†

---

* Historical Dictionary, article D'Alembert.
† Barruel's Memoirs, Vol. I. Chap. 18.

Chapter IV.

Occult Masonry

B Y Occult Masonry is here to be understood those Lodges of Free Masons, which, leaving their original simple institutions, introduced subjects and practices which had no connection with Masonry, and of which the lodges which remained pure, had no knowledge.*

To exhibit a brief view of what may be collected of importance respecting these adulterated Lodges, from Robison's Proofs and Barruel's Memoirs, is the design of this chapter. Such a view is a necessary introduction to the history of Illuminism, and its connection with the Masonic orders.

Dr. Robison observes, that in the early part of his life he commenced an acquaintance with Masonry, which he

---

* The authorities on which Dr. Robison chiefly relies, to support his narrative (besides the original writings) are,

1. Grosse Absicht des Illuminaten Ordens.
2. Nachtrages (3) denselben.
3. Weishaupt's improved system.
4. Sytem des Illum. Ordens aus dem Original Schriften gezogen. Rob. p. 162.

Rev. Dr. J. Erskine, in a letter to a correspondent in New England, dated June 13, 1801, adds his testimony to the authenticity of the books, and most alarming facts to which Dr. Robison refers; and adds, "I am willing you should make what use of my letter you may think proper." [Manuscript Letter.]

considered as affording a pretext for spending an hour or two in decent conviviality.   That, though he had been successful in his Masonic career, and attained some distinguished degrees, yet he was induced to suspend his intercourse with the lodges, viewing Masonry as an unprofitable amusement, and in a degree inconsistent with the more serious duties of life. That while in this state of indifference respecting Free Masonry, his attention was awakened, and his curiosity exciting by some new circumstances, particularly by what he met with in a German work, called *Religions Begebenheiten,* i.e. *Religious Occurrences,* a periodical work, published by Professor Kœster of Geissen, which convinced him that Masonry was applied to purposes of which he had been wholly ignorant. That he found the lodges the haunts of many projectors in religion and politics, in direct opposition to that established rule in Masonry, *"That nothing of religion or politics shall ever be introduced into the lodges,"* and that pursuing the subject, he found associations rising out of these abuses, destructive of religion and society. In this work he professes the benevolent design of teaching mankind the danger resulting from these combinations; and lest the freedom with which he exposes these perverted lodges, should be considered as inconsistent with his Masonic engagements, he vindicates himself by observing, that he has not divulged the secrets of original Masonry, and that he is under no obligations to conceal its abuses, and new invented degrees.*

Abbe Barruel introduces the subject of Masonry by

---

* Introduction to Robison's Proofs. Dr. Robison, in a letter to a correspondent in America, dated Sept. 23, 1800, writes, that since the publication of his book, he has "greatly increased the body of his evidence, by means of many German publications;" but that his ill health and official duties, prevent his arranging and publishing this evidence.

bearing a most honorable testimony of many lodges, in England in particular, whose members he considers as ignorant of the real object of the institution, which he pronounces to be radically evil. In support of this idea he attempts to prove, that the words *liberty and equality,* which are common to all lodges, imply, not simply that *Masonic Fraternity* of which they are usually considered as expressive, but what they have been explained to intend in France, during the late revolution. A *liberty* or freedom from all religious and moral obligation; an equality subversive of all social order and subordination.

It cannot be expected that his observations on this subject should be introduced here, as they have no very intimate connection with the object of our present inquiry; but they who wish to become more fully acquainted with his laborious review and explanation of Masonic mysteries, may recur to the ninth and succeeding chapters in the second volume of his Memoirs. He was himself a Mason; and at the same time not subject to the customary bonds of secrecy. To explain what is so unusual, he relates, That at the time of his admission, Masonry had become so frequent in France, that the secret was less guarded; that upon a Masonic occasion, where all of the company, except himself, were Masons, and generally his acquaintance and intimate friends, he was urged to join them, and, in a manner, forced with them into the lodge; but, still refusing the proposed oath with great resolution, his firmness, it was said, proved him a Mason, and he was accordingly received with great applauses, and at that time advanced to the degree of Master. This gave him peculiar advantages for treating this subject, and he appears not to have made a dishonorable use of the privilege.*

---

* Barruel's Memoirs, Vol. II. p. 152, 155.

Whatever doubts may be entertained of his general theory, his investigation affords indubitable proofs of the accommodating nature of Masonic mysteries, and the pliancy to all the purposes of cabal and intrigue. Robison's Proofs forcibly impress the same idea. In England the lodge afforded a retreat to the adherents of the Stuarts, and was a covert for their meetings. In France it was made subservient to the views of the British Pretender. In the lodge of the *Maçon Parfait* is the following device: "A lion wounded by an arrow, and escaped from the stake to which he had been bound, with the broken rope still about his neck, is represented lying at the mouth of a cave, and occupied with mathematical instruments, which are lying near him. A broken crown lies at the foot of the stake." There can be little doubt but that this emblem alludes to the dethronement, the captivity, the escape, and asylum of James II, and his hopes of restoration by the help of the loyal brethren. Great use was also made of Masonry by the Church of Rome, for securing and extending her influence on the laymen of rank and fortune.*

But this prominent feature of Masonry, its accommodating nature, will more readily be perceived when we come to notice its easy coalescence with the designs of the Illuminees.

The abuses of Masonry, which we are not tracing, and which came to their full growth in the Illuminated lodges, appear to have originated in a natural spirit of inquiry, struggling with the restraints which the French government formerly imposed on a free discussion of religion and politics. Under the covert of a lodge, they found themselves liberated from a painful restraint, and experienced the pleasure of communicating sentiments in safety, which, in

---

* Robison's Proofs, p. 28, 31.

another place, would have exposed them to danger.

We need not be told that even innocent indulgences are liable to degenerate into the most pernicious habits. This truth was forcibly exemplified in the French lodges. A channel being once opened by which the heart could give vent to its feelings, the small stream soon became a torrent, affording a passage to every absurd, skeptical, and disorganizing idea, and which, in its final progress, not only demolished the superstructures which superstition and despotism had raised, but threatened to undermine the foundations of religion and society.

The pliant forms of Masonry were easily wrought into a compliance with the new views of the Masons. New explanations were given, and new degrees invented, which, while they gave pleasure by the air of mystery attending them, served as a veil to conceal from the young adept, a full view of the object towards which he was led. The veil was gradually removed, as his exercised organs were strengthened to endure the discovery.

We find a striking instance of the new explanations given to ancient symbols, in the degrees of *Chevaliers de l'Orient, and Chevaliers de l'Aigle*, which were once explained as typical of the life and immortality brought to light by the gospel; but a more modern explanation represents the whole history and peculiar doctrines of the gospel, as being typical of the final triumph of reason and philosophy over error.

To meet the new views of the Masons, a new series of degrees was added to the list, viz. the *Novice*, the *Elû de la Verite*, and the *Sublime Philosophe*. A lively imagination would be gratified by tracing these curious allegories; but the reader must be satisfied with one as a sample; that of the *Chevalier de Soleil*, with was an early addition to the Masonic degrees. I have the rather chosen this instance, as here

Robison and Barruel appear not to harmonize in their relation. This apparent disagreement, however, vanishes upon a closer inspection, which will show us that they describe different parts of the same degree,

Robison confines himself to the introductory formula, in which we are to observe, that the *Tres Venerable* is Adam; the Senior Warden is Truth; and all the Brethren are Children of Truth. In the process of reception, brother Truth is asked, What is the hour? He informs father Adam, that among men it is the hour of darkness, but that it is mid-day in the lodge. The candidate is asked, Why he has knocked at the door, and what is become of the eight companions? He says, that the world is in darkness, and his companions and he have lost each other; that Hesperus, the star of Europe, is obscured by clouds of incense, offered up by superstition to despots, who have made themselves gods, and have retired into the inmost recesses of their palaces, that they may not be recognized to be men, while their priests are deceiving the people, and causing them to worship these divinities.*

Barruel's account of this degree, contains an explanation of the implements which the newly received brother finds in the lodge, and the instructions there given him. A part of these instructions, which succeed the foregoing introductory explanations, follow.

"By the *Bible* you are to understand, that you are to acknowledge no other law than that of Adam, the law that the Almighty engraved on his heart, and that is what is called the *law of nature*. The *compass* recalls to your mind, that God is the central point of every thing, from which every thing is equally distant, and to which every thing is equally near. By the *square* we learn, that God has made *every thing equal;* and by the *Cubic stone*, that *all your*

---

* Robison's Proofs, p. 33, 35.

actions are equal with respect to the sovereign good."

The most essential part of this discourse is that which brother Veritas (or Truth) gives of the degree of the Elect. Among others is the following passage: "If you ask me what are the necessary qualities to enable a Mason to arrive at the center of real perfection, I answer that to attain it, he must have crushed the head of the serpent of worldly ignorance, and have cast off those prejudices of youth concerning the mysteries of the predominant religion of his native country. *All religious worship being only invented in hopes of acquiring power, and to gain in precedency among men; and by a sloth which covets, under the false pretence of piety, its neighbor's riches.* This, my dear brother, is what you have to combat; such is the monster you have to crush under the emblem of the serpent. *It is a faithful representation of that which the ignorant vulgar adore, under the name of religion."** Such doctrines need no comment.

With these new degrees and explanations, the French lodges appear to have undergone some new modifications with respect to their connection and correspondence with each other. The *Bienfaisants,* at Lyons, rose into high reputation. This lodge seems to have taken the lead in the disorganizing sentiments of the day, and was acknowledged as a parent lodge by several foreign societies. But the most distinguished, was the *Grand Orient,* at Paris. This may be considered, rather as a *Masonic Parliament,* composed of delegates from all the principal lodges, and in which Masonic concerns were ultimately determined. In 1782, this society had under its direction 266 improved lodges; the whole united under the Duke of Orleans as Grand Master, at least apparently, but really guided by the most profound adepts, who made use of his interest and influence to

---

* Barruel's Memoirs, Vol. II. p. 163.

promote their views, and then resigned him to that destruction, which was pronounced just, by the unanimous vote of mankind.*

While the lodges in France were passing this metamorphosis, those in Germany retained their original, simple constitutions, which they first received from England in 1716. It is remarkable that the Germans had been long accustomed to the *word*, the *sign*, and the *grip* of the Masons; and there are extant, and in force, borough laws, enjoining the masters of the Masons to give employment to journeymen who had the proper word and sign. But the first German lodge, was established at Cologne, in the year abovementioned.

The Germans, always fond of the marvelous, had attributed strange powers to Masonry, and been seeking, with their characteristic patience, the power of transmuting metals, of raising ghosts, and other wonderful secrets which they imagined were concealed in Masonic mysteries. This disposition had rendered them the dupes of Hunde, Johnson, Stark, and other adventurers who found their advantages in German credulity.

But about the year 1757, an entire revolution took place. Some French officers, then residing at Berlin, undertook to communicate to the Germans their refinements in Masonry. They could not resist the enchantment of the ribbons and stars with which the French had decorated the order. A Mr. Rosa, a French commissary, brought from Paris a complete wagon load of Masonic ornaments, which were all distributed before it had reached Berlin, and he was obliged to order another to furnish the lodges of that city. The Masonic spirit was revived throughout Germany: All were eager to hear and learn. New degrees were invented,

---

* Barruel's Memoirs, Vol. II. p. 239; and Robison's Proofs, p. 37, 48.

and Masonry underwent a general revolution. All proclaiming the excellencies of Masonry; while not one could
tell in what its excellency consisted; their zeal but served to
increase their confusion and disorder.

Those who believed that Masonic mysteries concealed
the wonderful powers of magic and alchemy, engaged, with
fresh zeal, in chase of the airy phantom; and fresh adventurers appeared, who, in their turn, raised and disappointed
the hopes of their admirers. Happy would it have been, had
no worse consequences ensued than the waste of their time
and money in the pursuit of these fooleries; but these
French instructors, together with their new forms and
degrees, had communicated new notions respecting government and religion, and introduced the custom of
haranguing on these subjects in the lodges. A close connection was formed between the French and some of the
German lodges, and the former were not unwilling to
communicate their new discoveries.   Philosophically
illuminated, the German adepts began to discern, that
religion was the slavery of the free born mind; that reason
was the only safe guide, and the only deity whom mankind
ought to worship; that the establishment of government
was the original sin; and emancipation from all legal
restraint, the true regeneration taught by Jesus Christ; and
which can be effected only by the wonderful power of those
two words, *liberty* and *equality.**

The reader, who has not been acquainted with the
history of modern philosophy, will hardly believe, perhaps,
that this is a serious statement of facts, or find it easy to
conceive that such absurdities were ever dignified with the
title of philosophy. But these sentiments are all to be found
in the code of the Illuminees; and to possess the mind with

* Robison's Proofs, p. 63, 75.

these sentiments, is the grand design of that system of policy expressed by Illuminism; the history of which will be given in the succeeding chapters.

It is proper to observe here, that at this time, Baron Knigge, resided in the neighborhood of Frankfort, who from his youth had been an enthusiast in Masonry, and a believer in its cabalistic powers. Despairing, at length, of ever finding the Philosopher's Stone, in pursuit of which his father had spent his fortune, and he his time, his enthusiasm was now diverted into another channel. The skeptical discourses delivered in the lodges, assisted him to discover that Masonry was pure natural religion, and that the whole duty of man was comprised in Cosmopolitism, or sacrificing all private interests for the promotion of universal happiness. Inflamed with these romantic ideas, he labored to propagate them through the lodges.

The authority assumed by the lodges of Berlin, had disgusted many of their brethren, and produced divisions, which were further increased by a variety of adventurers, each of which had his adherents. The Baron, found these circumstances a bar to his success, for the removal of which he projected a general congress from all the Masonic societies in Europe and America. The deranged situation of Masonic concerns seemed to render such a meeting expedient; and by the assistance of the lodges of Frankfort and Wetzlar it was obtained, and held at Willemsbad, in 1780. Here deputies, assembled from the four quarters of the globe, were busied for six months, debating about the mysteries of Masonry with all the seriousness of state ambassadors.

While Knigge was laboring to possess the deputies with his sentiments, he was met by another Mason, the Marquis of Constanza, who convinced him that his new ideas respecting Masonry had been reduced to a regular system,

and were now rapidly spreading in several Masonic societies. Transported with this discovery, he eagerly united
himself to the Illuminees, which was the sect to which the
Marquis introduced him, and joined his efforts with those
of his new instructor to gain over deputies, and to give a
direction to the proceedings of the convention favorable to
the designs of the Illuminees.

In these attempts they were not without success.
Numbers entered fully into their views, and the general
result of the congress was agreeable to their wishes. It was
decreed, that any Mason of the three first degrees should be
admitted to every lodge of whatever description; which
opened all the lodges to the agents of Illuminism. It was
also decreed, that every lodge should have the liberty of
declaring to which grand lodge it would be subject. The
plan of union was termed Eclectic, which was also favorable
to the new order, as it was in lodges of that denomination
that began its existence.*

We shall now proceed to take a view of that memorable
society, in which all the Anti-Christian, and Anti-Social
opinions of the day were reduced to a regular system, and
propagated with a zeal worthy of a better cause.

---

* Robison's Proofs, p. 76, 83. Barruel's Memoirs, Vol. IV. p. 101, 104.

I lately met with the following remark, in a letter from Professor
Ebeling, which I beg leave to introduce for the satisfaction of those who
may be disposed to doubt the above representation of Germanic
Masonry. "Masonry (he writes) was much in vogue in Germany from
the year 1740 to 1760, but made no noise; but in later years the Masonry
of Germany was strangely corrupted; divisions arose, of which Robison
speaks pretty exact as far as I know."

Chapter V.

Illuminism. Its Origin, Actors, and different Grades

T H E lodge Theodore, of Munich in Bavaria, was the most remarkable of the Eclectic lodges; and had formed a constitution of its own, in consequence of instructions received from the lodge Bienfaisants in Lyons. Distinguished among the members of this lodge, was Dr. Adam Weishaupt, Professor of Canon Law in the University at Ingolstadt. He had acquired a high reputation in his profession, which drew around him numbers from the neighboring Universities. The advantages which these circumstances gave him for impressing his own views upon the minds of youth, perhaps first suggested to him the idea of becoming the leader of a more numerous society, and it certainly was the means of his success in spreading his pernicious sentiments.

The bold opinions in religion and politics, which were more openly taught in the lodge Theodore than in any other, and which Knigge labored to propagate, Weishaupt was the first to reduce to a regular code. His scheme appears to be calculated, not so much for uniting persons of similar sentiments in one society, as for seducing those of opposite inclinations, and by a most artful and detestable process, gradually obliterating from their minds every moral and religious sentiment. It is in this view principally that this plan of seduction calls for the attention of man-kind, as it develops the secret, insidious policy by which the agents of faction and infidelity lead on their disciples, still concealing their real designs, until the mind is involved in a maze of error, or entangled in snares from which there is no retreat.

Another trait which deserves particular notice in this prime theory of deception, is that artful structure by which the deluded victim is led to give his support to a system, which, in its invisible operation, is undermining the object of his fondest attachment. Persons have subscribed to this constitution who, had they been aware of its tendency and issue, would sooner have committed their hand to the flame.*

What those particulars were in Weishaupt's early life, which were confessedly "great deviations from pure moral-ity," we are not told; but the history of his illuminated career, and his conduct while he sustained the dignified office of a professor in a University, certainly give us no favorable idea of that part of his life, which is acknowledged to be immoral.

We here lay before the reader a letter, found among the original writings of the Illuminees in Bavaria, from Wei-shaupt to Hertel Canon of Munich, but under the feigned names of *Spartacus* to *Marius*.

SEPTEMBER, 1783.
    Now let me, under the most profound secrecy, lay open the situation of my heart; I am almost des-perate. My honor is in danger, and I am on the eve of losing *that reputation which gave me so great an authority over our people. My sister-in-law is with*

---

* Robison's Proofs, p. 82, 85. Barruel's Memoirs, Vol. III. Chap. 1.

child. How shall I restore the honor of a person who is the victim of a crime that is wholly mine? *We have already made several attempts to destroy the child;* she was determined to undergo all; but Euriphon is too timid. Could I depend on Celse's secrecy, (Professor Buder at Munich) he could be of great service to me; *he had promised me his aid three years ago.* Mention it to him if you think it proper. If you could extricate me from this unfortunate step, you would restore me to life, to rest, to honor, and to authority. If you cannot, I forewarn you of it, *I will hazard a desperate blow,* for I neither can nor will lose my honor. I know not what devil * * * [Here decency obliges us to be silent.] It is not too late to make an attempt, for she is only in her fourth month. Do think of some means which can extricate me from this affair.

I am yours,

SPARTACUS

Other letters to different persons upon the same subject, and of a similar import, were found with this. Though he had solemnly denied his ever having used, or even been acquainted with means of abortion; yet, when the matter became public, he admits the facts respecting his sister-in-law, and the attempt to destroy the child, but justifies himself with an effrontery which discovers still more than the crime itself, a mind lost to every sentiment of goodness. "This, he says, is far from proving any depravity of heart. In his condition, his honor at stake, what else was left him to do? His greatest enemies, the Jesuits, have taught, that in such a case it is lawful to make way with the child. In the introductory fault, he has the example of the best of men. The second was its natural consequence; it was altogether involuntary; and, in the eye of a philosophical judge, who does not square himself by the harsh letters of a blood thirsty lawgiver, he has but a very trifling account to settle."*

In connection with the character of the founder of the sect, it may be proper to bring into view, those of his Areopagites, in whom he principally confided, and who were seated next himself in the government of the society. He himself furnishes the portrait in a letter to Cato, (Zwack.)

"I have received," he writes, "the most fatal intelligence from Thebes. They have given a public scandal, by admitting into the lodges that vile *Propertius,* a libertine, loaded with debts, and a most detestable being. Our *Socrates,* who could be of the greatest use to us, is always drunk; our *Augustus* has acquired the worst of reputations; the brother *Alcibiades* is perpetually sighing and pining away at the feet of his handlady; *Tiberius* attempted to lay violent hands on Diomede's sister, and suffered himself to be caught by the husband; *Heavens! what men have I got for Areopagites!*"

It appears that it was not the detestable nature of these actions which excited his disgust, but their influence on the reputation of his order, for he further writes, "Judge yourselves what would be the consequence, if such a man as our Marcus Aurelius (Feder) were once to know what a *set of men, destitute of morals; what a set of debauchees, liars, spendthrifts, braggadocios, and fools, replete with vanity and pride, you have among you, &c.*"†

From several expressions in his letters, it appears that Weishaupt had, for a considerable time, been meditating the plan of an order which should in time govern the world; but it was not fully completed when he first put his system in operation, and instituted the *order of the Illuminees.* This

---

* Robison's Proofs, p. 130 to 134. Barruel's Memoirs, Vol. III. Chap. 1.
† Robison's Proofs, p. 114.

was done in May, 1776, by the initiation of two of his
University pupils; but the order was not fully established till
1778.*

Weishaupt's aim in the frequent reviews and nice
touches which he gave his plan, was first, to explore every
avenue of the heart, every process by which he might most
effectually seduce, and lead men blindfold; and in the next
place, to provide sufficiently for his own security; for,
notwithstanding the sentence of banishment which he was
under drew from him the most grievous complaints of
despotic cruelty, he considered it a much lighter punishment than that which awaited him in case of detection.

In a letter to Cato, he writes, "I daily put to the test what
I made last year, and I find that my performances of this
year are far superior. You know the situation in which I
stand. It is absolutely necessary that I should, during my
life, remain unknown to the greater part of the adepts
themselves. *I am often overwhelmed with the idea that all my
meditations, all my services and toils are, perhaps, only
twisting a rope, or planting a gallows for myself.*"†

The following scheme exhibits the different grades
through which the candidate progresses to the perfection of
Illumination.

NURSERY. {
Preparation,
Novice,
Minerval,
Illumin. Minor.

---

* Robison's Proofs, p. 107. Barruel's Memoirs, Vol. III. Chap. 1. Ibid.,
Vol. IV. p. 55, 56.
† Barruel's Memoirs, Vol. III. p. 12.

MASONRY.	Symbolic.	Apprentice, Fellowcraft, Master.
	Scotch.	Illum. Major, Novice, Illum. Dirigens, Knight.
MYSTERIES.	Lesser.	Presbyter, Priest, Prince, Regent.
	Greater.	Majus, Rex.*

There is a part common to all these degrees, viz. that of the Insinuator, or Recruiter; the duty of whose office is to find and bring forward members for the first and succeeding degrees.†

---

* Ibid., p. 19.
† Robison's Proofs, p. 139.

Chapter VI.

The Code of the Illuminees

I T was necessary that some members of the order should be known as such, that they might serve as guides to those who should have a desire to be initiated. These are the *Minervals,* who are the only visible members of the society. A candidate for admission must make his wish known to some Minerval; he reports it to a superior, by whom, in an appointed channel, it is communicated to the council. No farther notice is taken of it for some time. The candidate is observed in silence, if judged unfit for the order no notice is taken of his request; but if otherwise, he receives privately an invitation to a conference, and upon signing the declaration required of the preparation class, is admitted to the Novitiate.*

But the *Insinuators* are the principal agents for propagating the order. These are invisible spies, *seeking whom they may devour,* who enter on their tablets, with which they are always to be furnished, the names of such as they judge would be useful to the order, with the reasons for or against their admission.

The directions of the insinuator teach him to seek after young men from eighteen to thirty, those in particular who have not completed their education, and those whose

---

* Robison's Proofs, p. 94.

exterior prepossesses one in their favor. His attention is likewise directed to men of rank, wealth, and influence. Men of an insinuating, intriguing disposition, mechanics of all professions, booksellers, school masters, post masters, those who keep post houses, and the discontented of every class of people.

Of these minutes the Insinuator is required to make a return twice every month to his superiors, who form a list of such as they judge suitable prey, and put it into the hands of an Insinuator, not the one perhaps who sent in the name, but one whom the superiors of the order shall see fit to appoint. And he now begins the labor of gaining over his pupil to the society. The person thus marked as the object of seduction, though he has expressed no desire of uniting with the order is placed in the grade of

Preparation. It would be a task indeed to trace minutely the arts of insinuation, and the cautious steps by which the Recruiter is to proceed. In general, the curiosity of the subject is to be excited by suggestions, made as by accident, of the existence and power of such a society; his mind is to be impressed with the most honorable views of the design of this institution; his affections and confidence are to be gained by every art of insinuation; the power of secret societies, and the pleasure of secretly reigning, are to be presented to his imagination, and books provided by the society, and corresponding with its views, are to be put into his hands. Should he break from all these snares, he is marked for an enemy whose character and influence the society is henceforth concerned to destroy. *They must be gained, or ruined in the public opinion, it is the law of the order.* But should the candidate, by these arts, be led to express a desire to join this invisible combination, he is required to subscribe an express and solemn declaration, "never to reveal, by sign, word, or any other way, even to the most intimate friend, whatever shall be entrusted to him relative to his entrance into a secret society, and this whether his reception takes place or not; and that he subjects himself to this secrecy the more willingly, *as his introducer assures him, that nothing is ever transacted in this society hurtful to religion, morals, or the state.*"* The candidate having subscribed this declaration commences

Novice. He is now introduced to an instructor, the only one perhaps of the order whom he is permitted to know. By this instructor he is taught, *that silence and secrecy are the very soul of the order,* and enjoined never to speak of anything belonging to it, even before those whom he may suppose to be initiated, without the strongest necessity. He is also furnished with a new supply of books and writings, calculated for his advancement.

Here a cautionary direction is introduced, which extends to all the different degrees, that if any of the brotherhood fall sick, the other brethren are to visit him, to prevent his making any unfavorable declarations, and to secure any papers with which he may have been entrusted.

To qualify the Novice for the practice of that secrecy which has been represented as of such importance, he is furnished with what may be called the *Dictionary of Illuminism.* He here learns that no brother bears the same name in the order which he does in the world. He receives a name for himself, and is made acquainted with that of his instructor, and with those of the other brethren, as he is admitted to know them.

The following is a brief sample of this vocabulary. The fictitious name of Weishaupt, was *Spartacus;* of Knigge, *Philo;* of the Marquis Constanza, *Diomedes;* of Zwack, *Cato;* of Baron Bassus, *Hannibal;* of Count Saviloi, *Brutus;* of

---

* Robison's Proofs, p. 94. Barruel's Memoirs, Vol. III. Chap. 3.

Nicolai, *Lucian;* of Count Massenhausen, *Ajax;* of Councilor Hoheneicher, *Alcibiades;* or Merz, *Tiberius;* &c.*

The Novice is also put upon the study of a new *Geography,* from which he learns that places, as well as persons, bear a new name. Bavaria, is denominated *Achaia,* and Austria *Egypt;* Munich is called *Athens,* and Vienna, *Rome,* &c.

Time too, he finds, has undergone a new arrangement, and he must again study his calendar. The Persian era, beginning A. D. 630, is adopted by the Illuminees. The months are known by new names, and are of different lengths; Pharavardin has no less than forty-one days, while Asphandar has only twenty.

Nor is the candidate yet qualified to correspond with his new brethren, until he has acquired the cipher of the order. A simple one is prepared for the lower grades, but the superiors make use of hieroglyphics.

He now begins the study of the statutes of the society, and a morality extracted from heathen writers; but is told that the knowledge of mankind is above all other things important, and to acquire this, tracing characters, and noticing occurrences, are strenuously recommended; his observations are to be submitted to the review of his superiors.

In this stage of his novitiate, he is required to present the order with a written account of his name, place of birth and residence, age, rank, profession, favorite studies, books, secret writings, revenues, friends, enemies, parents, &c. A similar table is prepared by his instructor, of whatever he has been able to discover; and from a comparison of these, and his answers to a number of interesting questions, the

---

* Barruel's Memoirs, Vol. III. Chap. 4. and Vol. IV. p. 173. Robison's Proofs, p. 160.

superiors judge of the expediency of admitting him to the last proofs.

His admission being agreed upon, in the dead of night he is led to a gloomy apartment, and being repeatedly questioned respecting his readiness to devote himself to the order, he confirms his consent with a solemn oath, of which the following is a part, "*I vow an eternal silence, an inviolable obedience and fidelity to all my superiors, and to the statutes of the order. With respect to what may be the object of the order, I fully and absolutely renounce my own penetration and my own judgment.* I promise to look upon the interests of the order as my own; and as long as I shall be a member of it, *I promise to serve it with my life, my honor, and my estates.*" Having signed this oath, and with a sword pointed at his breast, being threatened with unavoidable vengeance, from which no potentate on earth can defend him, should he betray the order, he commences

Minerval, and becomes a member of a lodge.* Here Illuminism commences its connection with Masonry; and here those, who do not discover a disposition fully compliant with the views of their guides, are left to divert themselves with the three degrees of apprentice, fellowcraft, and master, and never attain any further acquaintance with Illuminism. But this, it was found, would not satisfy all candidates, and in particular, those who had previously been members of lodges; some intermediate degrees were therefore added, as the minor and major Illuminee, and Scotch Knight.

The Minervals hold frequent meetings under the direction of some more illuminated superior. These meetings are professedly devoted to literary pursuits, but particular care is taken to give the discussions a direction

---

* Barruel's Memoirs, Vol. III. Chap. 4.

which shall coincide with the designs of Illuminism. *That suicide is lawful under pressing dangers and calamities; that the end sanctifies the means,* or that theft and murder become commendable when committed to advance a good cause, are sentiments frequently brought into view in the meetings of the Minervals. From these discussions the superiors judge of the propriety of advancing the candidate to the next degree, which is that of*

Illuminatus Minor. The members of this class have meetings similar to those of the former degree, but their instructors are taken only from among those who have attained the rank of priest, and who are directed to labor to remove what, in the language of Illuminism, is termed political and religious prejudices. The candidates are now to be formed for useful laborers. They are put upon study-ing the secret arts of controlling the mind, of seizing the favorable moment, of discovering and addressing the ruling passion, or acquiring a pliancy and versatility of address, and of concealing their views and feelings from others. As they are found qualified, they have more or less of the minerval degree committed to their inspection.

Previous to his advancement to the next degree, the candidate is subjected to another scrutinizing examination respecting his views, and devotedness to the interests of Illuminism. He is likewise required to give the order a new proof of his confidence, by exhibiting an exact record of his whole life written without reservation. The design of the Institutor in requiring this, appears from his own remarks on this part of his code; *"Now I hold him; if he should wish to betray us, we have also his secrets."*

The history which the candidate gives of himself, is compared with the one already formed, in the records of the

---

* Robison's Proofs, p. 98. Barruel's Memoirs, Vol. III. Chap. 5.

order, from the returns made by his Instructor, and the discoveries of invisible spies, in which, everything relating to his character, abilities, weaknesses, passions, prospects, attachments, aversions, education, and even language, gait, and physiognomy, are noticed in perhaps fifteen hundred particulars. To impress the mind of the adept with the strongest sense of the activity of the order, and the folly of expecting to escape its vigilance, this portrait of himself is put into his hands, and he is again questioned respecting his disposition to unite with such a society.

The disposition of the candidate being sounded by a new series of questions, and having been repeated the former oaths of secrecy, and devotedness to the order, he passes through the initiating forms, by which means he becomes*

Illuminatus Major, or Scotch Novice. It is impossible, I find, in this brief sketch, to give a full view of the slow, artful, and insidious process by which the mind is powerfully, though insensibly, drawn from the possession of its former principles, and fired with a fanciful idea of soon attaining the regions of sublime wisdom.

The adept has still an Instructor, who now calls him to attend to the miseries under which mankind are groaning, and the inefficacy of all the means used for their relief. This is attributed to the restraints to which they are subjected by princes and the priesthood. The importance of *surrounding the powers of the earth with invisible agents, and insensibly binding their hands,* and the necessity of union among the friends of suffering humanity, to accomplish this desirable end, are strongly inculcated. The tractable pupil has but one grade more to ascend before he enters the secrets of

---

* Robison's Proofs, p. 102-106. Barruel's Memoirs, Vol. III. Chap. 6 and 7.

Illuminism. This is termed by the sect the*

Scotch Knight. In the late Masonic revolution, this new degree, which had been brought from France, was adopted by several of the German lodges. The welcome reception which those of this degree met with in all the lodges, determined the Illuminees to unite it with their system. This becomes a *Sta bene,* or stationary degree, to such as they see fit to advance above the common degrees of Masonry, but are not judged worthy of being admitted to the higher secrets.

Instead of the scenes of darkness and horror which attended the introduction to the other degrees, the candidate is now introduced into a splendid lodge, where all the Knights are present in the habiliments of their order; and here, he is told, is a part of those unknown legions, united by indissoluble bands, to defend the cause of humanity.

In the course of the ceremonies, *Jesus Christ is declared to be the grand master of the order,* the enemy of superstition, and asserter of reason; and in commemoration of him, a mock representation is exhibited of the Lord's Supper.

The instructions given the new Knight, direct him to promote the increase of Eclectic Masonry; to endeavor to gain an ascendancy in all other Masonic lodges, either to reform or destroy them; and, as far as possible, to convert their funds to the advancement of the cause of Illuminism.†

Here we come to the door which leads to the mysteries of Illuminism; and here we must leave behind all those, who, though pleased with romantic ideas of Cosmopolitism, and of undermining what appeared to them superstition, and who, under these impressions, might actively discharge the instructions last received, yet were not to be

---

* Barruel's Memoirs, Vol. III. Chap. 7.

† Proofs, p. 141 to 145. Memoirs, Vol. III. Chap. 8.

trusted with the higher mysteries of Illuminism.

The reader will naturally conclude, that all who were admitted to this order, were not subjected to these tedious preparatory forms; some were found (as Knigge for instance) who met the warmest wishes of the society, and without any preparation were introduced to its mysteries.

Chapter VII.

The Mysteries and Government of the Order

W E must not expect, on entering these secret chambers, to find the veil which conceals the real design of the Illuminees wholly removed. The terrifying impressions of the rope, which Weishaupt was so conscious of meriting, kept him much behind the curtain. This induced him to divide his mysteries into the *lesser* and the *greater,* each of which have two departments, one relating chiefly to Religion, and the other to Politics. The first degree in the lesser mysteries is that of the

Edopt, or *Priest.* As introductory to this degree, several questions are proposed to the candidate, which imply, that no religion, government, or civil association on earth corresponds with the wants of mankind; and that secret societies are the safe, only effectual remedies to supply this defect. He is asked, and the question merits the consideration of those who ridicule the apprehension of danger from Illuminism, *"Have you any idea of secret societies; of the rank they hold, or the parts they perform in the events of this world? Do you view them as insignificant and transient meteors?* O brother! God and Nature had their admirable ends in view, and they make use of these secret societies as the only, and as the indispensable, means of conducting us thither. *These secret schools of philosophy shall one day retrieve the fall of human nature, and princes and nations shall disappear from the face of the earth, and that without any violence. Reason shall be the only book of laws, the sole code of man."*

The object of the secret of Jesus, he is told, was to reinstate mankind in the original liberty and equality, but that this secret was disclosed only to a few. In proof of this he quotes these words of Christ. "To you is given to know the mystery of the kingdom of God; but to them that are without, all things are done in parables."*

This doctrine, the proselyte is then told, is the origin of Masonry, and the true explanation of its hieroglyphics. The rough stone of Masonry, is the symbol of the primitive state of man, savage, but free. The stone split, represents the state of fallen nature, of mankind divided according to their states, governments, or religions.

On this occasion the proselyte, previous to his receiving the priestly unction, is vested with a white tunic; the sleeve is tied at the extremity and middle with bandages of scarlet, and he wears a broad silken belt of the same color. This dress is particularly described, because it was in a similar one that, during the French revolution, a comedian appeared personally attacking Almighty God, saying, "No! thou dost not exist. If thou hast power over the thunder bolts, grasp them; aim them at the man who dares set thee at defiance in the face of thy altars. But no, I blaspheme thee, and I still live. No, thou dost not exist."† The next degree in the lesser mysteries is that of the

Regent. As preparatory to the introduction of the candidate to this degree, he is brought to the lodge in the habit of a slave loaded with chains. "It is inquired, who

---

* Mark, iv. 11.
† Proofs, p. 145 to 151. Memoirs, Vol. III. Chap. 10.

reduced him to that most miserable of all conditions? It is answered, society, governments, the sciences, and false religion. A voice from within denies him entrance, declaring, that none but freemen can enter here. His guide then answers for him, that his will is to be free; that he has been illuminated; flies from his tyrants, and seeks refuge among freemen."

It is needless to detail the hackneyed sentiments found in the instructions given on this occasion, as, excepting the mode of expressing them, they are very similar to those which have already been mentioned, and which will be found in their private correspondence less veiled in mystery.

One part of these instructions, however, arrests the attention, which follows; "The great strength of our order lies in its concealment; let it never appear in any place in its own name, but always covered by another name, and another occupation. *None is fitter than the three lower degrees of Free Masonry; the public is accustomed to it, expects little from it, and therefore takes little notice of it. Next to this, the form of a literary society is best suited to our purposes.*"

Upon the admission of the Regent, his former oaths and secrets are relinquished, with an expression of entire confidence in his firmness; and in return he gives the order an instrument, legally executed, by which they are empowered, in case of his decease, to claim any private papers with which he may be entrusted.*

Such were the lesser mysteries of the Illuminees. Those which they term the greater, were likewise distinguished into those of *Majus,* or Philosopher, and *Rex,* or Man King. These degrees were not found with the other writings; and the cause appears in a letter from Spartacus (Weishaupt) to Cato, in which, speaking of one of his higher degrees, he

---

* Proofs, p. 151 to 154. Memoirs, Vol. III. Chap. 11, 15.

says, "I never suffer it to go out of my hands. *It is of too serious an import.*" Philo, (Knigge) who it seems assisted in forming the higher degrees, writes to the same person; "I have made use of such precaution in the degrees of Edopt, and of Regent, that I should not be afraid of conferring them on Kings or Popes, provided they have undergone the proper previous trials. In our last mysteries we have acknowledged this *pious fraud.*"*

Dr. Robison here quotes the publisher of the Neueste Arbitung, and Grollman; and Abbe Barruel quotes Biederman, and a writer, who had left his name with the editors of the Eudemonia, (a Journal printed at Frankfort-on-the-Main) to be published if necessary, who all profess to have read these degrees, and unite in their testimony, "that in the degree of *Majus* the doctrines are the same with those of Spinoza, where all is material. God and the world are the same thing, and all religions are represented as chimerical, and the invention of ambitious men." The second degree, or *Rex*, teaches, "that every citizen, or householder is a sovereign, as in the Patriarchal state; that all authority, and all magistracy must be destroyed, and that democratic governments are not more consonant with nature than any others."†

The reader doubtless will remark the inconsistency between these sentiments upon government, and the attempt which Weishaupt was then making to render the government of the Illuminees universal and absolute. All that appears to remove this inconsistency, is to be found under the degree of Regent, where, in a series of questions, the candidate is led to say, "That mankind ought to think themselves happy in having *superiors of tried merit;* and

---

* Barruel's Memoirs, Vol. III. Chap. 12.
† Proofs, p. 158. Memoirs, Vol. III. Chap. 12., and Note.

who, unknown to each other, could not possibly support each other in treasonable combinations against the general welfare; and that, supposing *despotism* were to ensue, it *could not be dangerous* in the hands of men, who from the very first step we took in the order, taught us nothing but *science, liberty, and virtue.*"*

Having thus traced the artful process by which Weishaupt led his disciples to expect, like the deluded parents of our race, *to become as Gods,* but which, in fact, was calculated to deprive them of light, truth, and righteousness; we here subjoin a brief view of the arrangement and governmental regulations of the society. At the head of the order, however extensive, is the

General; to whom regular returns are to be made of whatever relates to its general, or more particular interests. A constant communications and correspondence is to be preserved between him and the

Areopagites, or council of twelve, who compose the next degree in the general government. The General of the order is to be elected by this council, and from their own number, and to them only is he known, except to such immediate confidants, agents, and secretaries as he shall see fit to employ. The business of this supreme council is to receive the returns that are made, and prepare them for the inspection of the General; and they are particularly directed to "project and examine plans to be adopted for gradually enabling the society to attack the enemy of reason and human nature, *personally.*" Next in the office is the

National Director; who sustains the same relation to the Illuminees of a particular nation, which the General does to the whole order. The views of the society were not confined to one nation. He too, as the General, has his council of

---

* Barruel's Memoirs, Vol. III. p. 133.

twelve.* Subordinate to him are the

Provincials, who have the direction of the affairs of the order in the several provinces. The Provincial is empowered to assemble such regents of his providence as he shall choose to assist in council.† The next in dignity, though not in the direct line of the general arrangement, is the

Dean. He is chosen by the Epopts, and presides in their academy. The

Epopts, or *Priests,* form a curious and important part in the general system. From this class is formed an academy or chamber of science, consisting of their most learned men in the various arts and sciences. The persons composing this academy, were to be supported by the funds of the society, that they might devote their time to the objects of their appointment. All questions of difficulty proposed by any of the inferior degrees, were to be required to be given in writing, to their immediate superiors, and by them transmitted to the academy for solution; from thence, in the same channel, the querist received his answer, but from a source to him unknown. The reader will observe the tendency of this institution to promote the literary reputation of the order, and to persuade the adept that he is connected with the fountain head of science.

"*The Occult Sciences,*" form one branch particularly recommended to the attention of the academy, under which is comprehended "The study of the oriental tongues, and others little known; secret methods of writing, and the art of deciphering; *the art of raising the seals of the letters of others,* and of preserving their own from similar practices; the study of ancient and modern hieroglyphics, of secret

---

* Barruel's Memoirs, Vol. III. Chap. 18.
† Barruel's Memoirs, Vol. III. Chap. 17.

societies, Masonic systems, &c.* Subordinate to the Provincial, in a direct line, we find the

Prefects, each of which may have the inspection of eight lodges, in whose meetings they are required to preside. To these, principally, is entrusted the care of the lower part of the edifice.

The regents alone are eligible to the above offices; and those of this degree who have no particular appointments, are charged with the general inspection of the lower orders, and to study the advancement of the interests of the society by all possible means.

A degree of supervisorship and inspection is likewise committed to the Scotch Knights, and even to the Major and Minor Illuminees, over the Minerval, and other preparatory classes, but at the same time they themselves are under the constant inspection of Prefects and Regents, to whom alone the real views of the order are known.†

The instructions given to these several agents of Illuminism, would serve greatly to unfold the art, and discover the object, of the institution. They are a compound of whatever the highest machiavellian policy could suggest, to conceal, and yet advance the ends of the subtle projector, and to acquire and maintain a tyrannical ascendancy over the minds of men; but they are too numerous to be introduced here.‡

Very just is that remark made by Professor Renner, one of the deponents on the subject, *That the great strength of the order consists in its invisibility.* A brother may know the secrets of his class, and those of an inferior one, but all above him are entirely unknown; unless his superiors have

---

* Barruel's Memoirs, Vol. III. Chap. 14.

† Barruel's Memoirs, Vol. III. Chap. 16.

‡ Ibid., p. 175-248.

conferred on him the commission of Director, Visitor, or Spy. The chiefs, by this method, watch an inferior, while they themselves are concealed; they know how far he is devoted to the order, and true to the secrets with which he is entrusted. If he has doubts, to whom can he reveal them with confidence, when the person to whom he commits himself, may be one employed to sift him, and who encourages his confidence only to betray him?

"An advantage still more important, results from this concealment, for should any one be disposed, he is incapable of discovering the superiors of the order, while they at the same time can give their support to any of the accused without suspicion, perhaps, of being connected with them."

This invisibility, as they call it, of the real Illuminees, it may be imagined excludes all communication from the lower to the superior degrees; whereas, in fact, any person belonging to the lower grades may exhibit a complaint against his Instructor, or ask any privilege of the Provincial, National, or General, according to his standing, while at the same time he remains wholly ignorant of the person he addresses, and even of the place of his residence. Indeed, the inferiors of the order are required to make, in this way, a monthly return to their invisible superiors, of the conduct of those under their inspection, and of whatever they conceive materially interesting to the institution.

This curious correspondence is conducted in the following manner: A letter, with the direction of *Quibus Licet*, i. e. to whom it belongs, and marked with the sign of the class of which the writer is a member, is opened by the next superiors. Those having the addition of *Soli* or *Primo*, are conveyed to the Provincial, National, or General, according to the rank of the writer, and the direction which is given, whether *Soli* or *Primo.**

---

* Robison's Proofs, p. 177. Barruel's Memoirs, Vol. III. p. 225., Vol. IV. p. 145 to 149.

Chapter VIII.

The Discovery of the Sect

THE first alarm was given by a discovery of many dangerous publications which were secretly circulated; several of these were traced back to lodge Theodore, of which Weishaupt was a member. Friendly remonstrances were first made by the Elector of Bavaria, on the subject, but these abuses continuing, he ordered a judicial inquiry into the proceedings of this lodge. It was found that this, and several associated lodges, were preparatory schools for another order of Masons, who denominated themselves *The Illuminated.* Several called Minervals, were said to belong to this order, but the persons, by whom they were admitted, were unknown. Some of these were privately examined by the Elector himself. They said they were bound to secrecy; but they assured the Elector, on their honor, that the aim of the order was useful both to church and state.

This not relieving the public anxiety, an order was published on the 22nd of June, 1784, forbidding all secret assemblies, and shutting up the Mason lodges. The members of the lodge Theodore distinguished themselves by a pointed opposition to this order; reprobating the prohibition as cruel, and continuing their meetings. By a subsequent edict, the order of the Illuminees was abolished, and search made, in the lodge Theodore, for papers; none of importance, however, were found.

In 1785, four Professors of the Marianen Academy, viz. Utschneider, Cosandey, Renner, and Grunberger, with some others, who appear to have withdrawn from the order, under a conviction of its evil tendency, were summoned before a court of inquiry. None of these had been admitted to the mysteries, yet their evidence was alarming. Their testimony agreed with what has been related respecting the lower degrees, and they further declared, "that, in the lodges, sensual pleasures were advocated, and self-murder justified, on Epicurean and stoical principals; that death was represented as *an eternal sleep;* patriotism and loyalty were called narrow-minded prejudices, incompatible with universal benevolence. Nothing was so frequently discussed as the propriety of employing, for a good purpose, the means which the wicked employed for evil purposes."

These depositions, given separately, under oath, and the signature of the deponents, were perfectly harmonious; but the most offensive parts were denied by the Illuminees, and much clamor was raised. Weishaupt, however, was deprived of his Professor's chair, and banished from Bavaria. He went first to Regensburg, and afterward entered into the service of the Duke of Saxe Gotha, whose name in the order was Timoleon.*

In 1786, a collection of original papers and correspondence, was found in the house of counselor Zwack; and soon after, a much larger collection in the castle of Sanderdorf, belonging to Baron Bassus. This collection has been published, by order of the Elector, under the title of *"Original Writings."* From these papers, principally, were taken the details respecting the code and government of the

---

* Robison's Proofs, p. 85 to 89. Barruel's Memoirs, Vol. IV. Chap. 7.

Illuminees.* Some extracts from the epistolary part of these writings will now be presented to the reader, more fully to bring into view the object of the order, and the means adopted to attain this object.

Spartacus, writing to Cato, on the subject of establishing a peculiar morality and religion, fitted for the great body of mankind, says, "But this is a ticklish project, and requires the utmost circumspection. The squeamish will start at the sight of religious and political novelties; and they must be prepared for them. We must be particularly careful about the books we recommend. I shall confine them at first to moralists, and reasoning historians. *Robinet, Mirabeau, the Social System, Natural Polity, the Philosophy of Nature,* and such works are reserved for our higher degrees. At present they must not even be mentioned to our adepts, and particularly *Helvetius on Man.*" The reader here sees a list of the most anti-religious, atheistical productions, and that they are reserved for the last mysteries. "Marius," he adds, "an excellent man, must be dealt with. His stomach, which cannot yet digest such strong food, must acquire a better tone."† But after all the cautious steps of the leader, Knigge, in a letter to Zwack, expresses his apprehensions, that *"such a superabundance of atheism would betray the tendency of the sect too soon."*‡

Brutus writes, "Numenius (Count Kollowrath) now acquiesces in the morality of the soul, but, I fear we shall lose Ludovicus Bavarus. He told Spartacus that he was mistaken when he thought he had swallowed his stupid Masonry."§

---

* Robison's Proofs, p. 107. Barruel's Memoirs, Vol. III. p. 145.
† Robison's Proofs, p. 109. Barruel's Memoirs, Vol. IV. p. 43.
‡ Barruel's Memoirs, Vol. IV. Observations, p. 8.
§ Robison's Proofs, p. 169.

Weishaupt, writing to Cato, an account of his degree of priests, says, "One would almost imagine, that this degree, as I have managed it, is real Christianity. In this sense, no man need be ashamed of being a Christian, for I preserve the name, and substitute reason."*

The Areopagites, though united in their object, appear to have differed much with respect to the best means of attaining it; while some were fearful of alarming the adepts by too hasty discoveries, other were disgusted with the tedious slowness of this process of deceit. Minos (Baron Dittfurt) "wanted to introduce atheism at once, and not go hedging in the manner they did; affirming, it was easier to show at once that atheism was friendly to society, then to explain all their Masonic Christianity, which they were afterwards to show to be *a bundle of lies.*"† Language cannot furnish a phrase, more descriptive than this, of the nature of Illuminism; the whole system was "a bundle of lies," a plan of concealed falsehood and deception. The means perfectly correspond with the design of the projectors, and sufficiently explain the nature of that design.

We have before been led to notice the importance which these conspirators attribute to secret societies, as .the mainspring of their destructive machinery. While they are perpetually reminding each other, that here lay their hopes of success, it becomes us not to lose sight of this engine of mischief. The following is an extract from a lecture, which Weishaupt read to his adepts on this subject. "When the object is universal revolution, all the members of these societies must find means of governing invisibly, and without any appearance of violence, men of all stations, of all nations, and of every religion. Insinuate the same spirit

---

* Robison's Proofs, p. 119. Barruel's Memoirs, Vol. III. p. 144.
† Robison's Proofs, p. 135.

everywhere. In silence, but with the greatest activity possible, direct the scattered inhabitants of the earth toward the same point." In proof of the importance of such a secret union, he reasons thus: "The slightest observation shows that nothing will so much contribute to increase the zeal of the members as secret union. We see with what keenness and zeal the frivolous business of Free Masonry is conducted by persons knit together by the secrecy of their union."*

Among their plans of deception was found a scheme "for a public literary academy, to consist of two classes of men; the one of men remarkable for their zeal in religion, the other of profound Illuminees. Each member to wear on his breast a medal with this inscription, *Religioni et Scientiis*," (to religion and sciences.)† *"And no marvel; for Satan himself is transformed into an angel of light."*

Spartacus, writing to Cato, says, "There must not a single purpose come in sight that is ambiguous, and that may betray our aims against religion and the state. That we may be uncontrolled in our discourse, let our pupils remark that the superiors enjoy great latitude in that respect; *that we sometimes speak in one way, and sometimes in another,* only to sound the opinions of those we converse with." This the pupil is told; but he is not told that the real design is, to secure a retreat, when they have incautiously gone too far; and to render their real sentiments impenetrable to their inferiors.‡

Among the instructions which Weishaupt gives his disciples, "he exhorts, and seriously admonishes those who have the care of rare books or precious manuscripts, in the

---

* Barruel's Memoirs, Vol. III. p. 18. Robison's Proofs, p. 93.

† Barruel's Memoirs, Vol. IV. Observation, p. 9.

‡ Ibid., Vol. III. p. 177. Robison's Proofs, p. 119.

libraries of princes, nobles, and religious orders, to take them for the benefit of those to whom they would be more useful." Sending a list of what he would have taken from the library of the Carmes, he says, *"all these would be of much greater use if they were in our hands. What do those rascals do with all those books?"*

Writing to Cato on the same subject he says, "Marius (keeper of the archives of the Electorate) has ferreted out a noble document, which we have got. He makes it, forsooth, a case of conscience. How silly that; since only that is *sin,* which is *ultimately* productive of mischief. In this case, where the advantage far exceeds the disadvantage, it is *meritorious virtue."**

But not satisfied with robbing mankind of their money and books, he contrived as unjustly to pilfer their fame, and appropriate to his order, their deserved reputation. At one time his direction is, "to endeavor to gain, or ruin every rising character." At another, he gives the Regents the following instructions; "It is very proper to make your inferiors believe, without telling them the real state of the case, that all other secret societies, particularly that of Free Masonry, are secretly directed by us. Or else, and it is really the fact in some states, that potent *monarchs* are governed by our order. When any thing remarkable or important comes to pass, hint that it originated with our order. *Should any person by his merit acquire a great reputation, let it be generally understood that he is one of us."*†

There was found in the handwriting of Zwack, a project for a sisterhood. It contains the following passages. "It will be of great service, and procure us much information and money, and will suit charmingly many of our truest mem-

---

* Robison's Proofs, p. 110. Barruel's Memoirs, Vol. III. p. 57.
† Barruel's memoirs, Vol. III. p. 204.

bers, who are the lovers of sex. It should consist of two classes, the virtuous and the freer hearted; they must not know each other, and must be under the direction of men, but without knowing it. Proper books must be put into their hands, and such (but secretly) as are flattering to their passions."

A list and description of eighty-five young ladies of Manheim, was found with this project. Minos makes an offer of his wife, and his four daughters-in-law to be the first adepts. "The eldest," he says, "is excellent. She is twenty-four, has read much, is above all prejudices, *and in religion, thinks as I do.*"

It appears that the institution of a lodge was attempted at Frankfort, and a discourse, as delicate as the sentiments of such men could conceive, was prepared for the occasion. After much of the tortuous eloquence of Illuminism, the orator thus address his fair assembly. "Rejoice in the dawn of Illuminism and freedom. Nature at last enjoys her sacred never fading rights. Long was her voice kept down by civil subordination; but the days of your majority now draw nigh, and you will no longer, under the authority of guardians, account it a reproach to consider with enlightened eyes the secret workshops of nature, and to enjoy your work and duty." Minos thought this very fine, but it raised a terrible disturbance, and broke up the assembly.*

Among these papers was likewise found the description of a strong box, which, if forced open, would blow up and destroy the contents; several receipts for procuring abortion; a composition which blinds or kills when thrown in the face; a method for filling a bedchamber with pestilential vapors; the secret of taking off and imitating the impression of seals, so as to use them afterwards; a collection of one-

* Robison's Proofs, p. 110, 137, 335. Barruel's Memoirs, Vol. III. p. 24.

hundred-thirty seals of princes, nobles, clergymen, mer-
chants, &c.; a receipt ad excitandum furorem uterinam; a
manuscript entitled, "Better than Horus," which contained
all the blasphemies of atheism; a dissertation on suicide:
also injunctions to all the superiors to learn to write with
both hands; and that they should use more than one cipher.

The reader, perhaps, will find it difficult to conceive how
this horrid artillery could be made conducive to the ends
which the order professed to have in view, the advancement
of religion, and social good. The Illuminees have furnished
us with a solution. "This apparatus," they said, "was with
propriety in the hands of counselor Zwack who was a judge
of a criminal court, and whose duty it was to know such
things." Admitting this, one thing still remains unac-
counted for, viz. how they come to be put with the papers of
the Illuminees?*

In consequence of these discoveries, some were deposed
from offices they sustained, and several banished. Apolo-
gies, and partial representations of Illuminism were published, and great was the outcry of cruelty which resounded
from all quarters; while others, imputed the lenity of
government on this occasion, to the invisible influence
which the order had gained over the measures of the
court.†

It appears that Illuminism had made a progress propor-
tionate to the zeal of the actors; Bavaria alone is said to have
contained about six hundred. Three of the witnesses above
mentioned declare, "that while connected with the order,
they were several times informed that it had extended to
Italy, to Venice, to Austria, to Holland, Saxony-on-the-
Rhine, and even to *America*." In the original writings

* Robison's Proofs, p. 111, 112. Barruel's Memoirs, Vol. IV. p. 167.
† Barruel's Memoirs, Vol. IV. Chap. 8.

several lodges in *America* are put on the list. This was before 1786.

A report respecting the progress of the order in Greece (Bavaria,) was found among the papers of Zwack, in his handwriting, which presents an alarming view of the prevalence of Illuminism, at a time when the public scarcely knew that the order was in existence. After mentioning a number of lodges, under the direction of the Illuminees, in several parts of the electorate, it is noted, "At Munich we have bought an house, and have taken our measures so well, that they even speak of us with esteem. This is a great deal for this city. We have a good museum of natural history, and apparatus for experiments. The garden is well occupied by botanic specimens, and the whole has the appearance of a society of zealous naturalists.

"The Dowager Duchess has set up her academy entirely according to our plan. All the Professors are of *our order* and all the pupils will be ours.

"On the recommendation of the brethren, *Pylades* is made the *ecclesiastical fiscal councilor,* and has the church money at his disposal. By properly using this money, we have already repaired the mal-administration of ——, and of ——, and have assisted more brethren under similar misfortunes.

"The brethren who are in orders have all been provided with livings and curacies, or with preceptor's places.

"All the German schools, and the benevolent societies, are at last under our direction.

"We shall shortly be masters of the Bartholomew institution for the education of *young ecclesiastics. By this means we shall be able to stock all Bavaria with priests both clever and proper.*

"We have at length got the remaining revenues of the Jesuits under the control of our order. This cost our senate some nights want of sleep."*

This discovery very much disconcerted the plans of the Illuminees, but it did not alter their habits or principles. Under a new name, and with new agents, we shall find them, in the following chapter, pursuing the same object, and we shall see the long train which infidelity has been preparing, kindled into an explosion which has changed the face of Europe, and been felt by remote nations.

He who habituates his mind to serious reflections, and is suitably disposed to derive instruction from the scenes around him, will find means of improvement, even among these disgusting objects. He will at least, feel his inactivity in a worthy cause reproved, by the labors, the zeal, the unremitting perseverance of these agents of destruction; for who can boast an equal engagedness, a mind equally awake to seize every opportunity and advantage, for promoting the cause of religion and the good of society, with what these men discover, in laboring for the destruction of both?

---

* Robison's Proofs, p. 155-159. Barruel's Memoirs, Vol. IV. p. 161, 57-59.

Chapter IX.

The German Union

A note, transmitted from Germany to England, appeared in the Monthly Magazine of January, 1798; in which the public were assured, "that from the beginning of the year 1790, every concern of the Illuminati has ceased, and no lodge of Free Masons in Germany, has, since that period, taken the least notice of them."* It is worthy of remark, that this certificate implicitly acknowledges, that until 1790, the Illuminees did exist, and were connected with the lodges of Free Masons in Germany; yet those, who endeavored to convince the public of their existence, at the time in which it is here acknowledged, were as contemptuously scouted, as those are, who now believe the subject important to mankind.

But are such men as Weishaupt and his coadjutors, thus easily beat off from their purposes? Do such Ethiopians so readily change their skin? No, Weishaupt himself has sufficiently, though unintentionally, warned us not to depend on such declarations. Writing to Cato, he says, "I have foreseen everything; I have prepared everything. Let my whole order go to rack and ruin; in three years I will answer to restore it, and that to a more powerful state than

---

* Barruel's Memoirs, Vol. IV. p. 180.

it was in before. Obstacles only stimulate my activity."*

How far he was active, after his banishment, in promoting the cause of Illuminism, does not appear, but a new confederation, on similar principals, and pursuing the same object, was formed, called the *German Union.* It was expedient that known Illuminees should take a less active part in this new arrangement. Probably the advice which was found in the handwriting of Cato, was adopted on this occasion, which was this: "In order to re-establish our affairs, let some of the ablest of those brethren, who have avoided our misfortunes, take the place of our founders."†

The Illuminees, in projecting this second part, appear to have taken their clue from the following existing circumstances. That scheme of religion, which excludes from the gospel all its *peculiarities,* had, for some time, been making a rapid progress in Germany. One excess led on to another, till doctrines were advanced among the clergy, which would leave the superiority of Christianity, to natural religion, very doubtful. This tendency to infidelity, appears to have been, in a great degree, owing to the influence of the Anti-Christian conspiracy, of which we have been speaking; but, however this may be, it was found to be a very convenient stock on which to ingraft a branch of Illuminism. An opportunity was now given, to such as wished to extirpate Christianity, to take part with those divines who were striving to explain away its distinguishing doctrines.

On these circumstances was founded the idea of the German Union. A multitude of writers appeared who expressed great zeal for Christianity; but the manifest object of this zeal was, to reduce it to a system of natural religion. The Bible was explained, corrected, allegorized, and other-

---

* Barruel's Memoirs, Vol. IV. p. 130.
† Barruel's Memoirs, Vol. IV. p. 178.

wise twisted, till the minds of men had hardly anything left to rest on, as a doctrine of revealed religion. This was a signal for others to come forward, deny revelation, and assert that man had no other ground of confidence that the dictates of natural reason. Another set of writers proceeding from this as a point already settled, proscribed all religion whatever, and openly taught the doctrines of materialism and atheism.* But it afterwards appeared, that these movements were the effects of combination and design, and that an association was formed who were unitedly striving to drive things to this extremity.

One Barth, a doctor of divinity in the university at Halle, was the principal agent in this combination. he was an Illuminee, and a person of most infamous morals. In this instance Mr. Ebeling acknowledges, that, "As to Barth, Robison is not very erroneous." But, even here, he appears much disposed to palliate, and tells us that "Barth did not write against religion; but only attempted to *modernize Christianity.*" He even seems to recommend his writings, from this consideration, that "He knew vice by *experience,* and could show all its deformity." Yet even Mr. Ebeling does not pretend that he ever ceased to love vice, or to practice it.

The dissoluteness of his morals had deprived him of the means of a decent subsistence, when, on a sudden, he purchased, near Halle, a large mansion, which he called Barth's ruhe. This became the headquarters of the Union. The management of this institution was committed to twenty-two conductors, whose agents were dispersed through the different towns. The persons chiefly sought after, were authors, postmasters, printers, and booksellers. While every encouragement was given to those works which

---

* Robison's Proofs, p. 66 to 72. Barruel's Memoirs, Vol. IV. p. 192 to 194.

favored their designs, it was found difficult, in some instances, to procure the publication of works designed to correct these evils. Every obstruction was given to the circulation of those of this description, which had come from the press; and funds were to be established to indemnify those booksellers, who, instead of selling such books, would conceal them in their shops.

But the principal means, on which they depended for corrupting the public mind, were *literary societies,* or *reading clubs;* which they labored to set up in every town. These were modifications of Weishaupt's minerval schools; they became very numerous; and it was the business of the secretaries, and initiated booksellers, to have them furnished with books of the most Anti-Christian character.

One of the vilest things, published on this occasion, was, the "Edict for Religion," written in derision of some regulations, published by the King of Prussia, under that title. This was traced to Barth's ruhe. He was thereupon arrested, his papers seized, and he imprisoned. This put a stop to the business of the Union; but Dr. Robison quotes persons *in high office at Berlin,* as agreeing in opinion, that the association of writers, and other turbulent persons in Germany, has been but very faintly hit by this blow, and is almost as active as ever.*

As Mr. Ebeling speaks in the most contemptuous manner, of Dr. Robison's *persons in high office at Berlin,* I beg leave to introduce here, the sentiments of some of that court upon the subject, and in particular, those of the king of Prussia, whom Mr. Ebeling mentions in the highest terms of respect, and ranks with the best of princes.

The Chevalier Von Hamelberg, a major in the king of Prussia's service, lately translated Dr. Robison's work into

---

* Proofs, p. 221 to 245. Memoirs, Vol. IV. p. 195 to 204.

PROOF OF THE ILLUMINATI

the German language, and presented a copy of the work to his sovereign, to which the king made the following return:

My dear Major Hamelberg,

The work which you have translated and communicated to me, with your letter of March 3rd, exposes the pernicious tendency of all secret societies in the clearest light, and is entitled to a considerable degree of merit with your countrymen. I, therefore, most willingly express my warmest satisfaction, and most sincere thanks, for the copy which has been transmitted to me, and I hereby announce my approbation of the work, as your affectionate king,

FREDERICK WILLIAM

CHARLOTTENBURG, *July* 25, 1800.

This was communicated to Dr. Robison, in a letter from major Hamelberg. This letter is so well calculated to throw light upon this subject, that I cannot refrain from introducing the more interesting parts of it.

SIR,

I have at last, after a long search, succeeded in my endeavors to obtain your valuable work on the secret societies, which was so thoroughly suppressed in *Germany,* that it was not possible to procure a copy of. As soon as I obtained it, I communicated it to some friends, as much distinguished by their character as by their talents; who, being all convinced of its excellence, persuaded me to translate it into German. As the whole merit of the work is yours, sir, I feel it to be my duty to send you the enclosed answer from the king my master. And should you be of the opinion that it will serve a good cause, you are at liberty to make any use of it which you may think proper. I think it necessary, sir, to apprize you that I have added some notes, and some facts which have come within my knowledge, and which evidently prove (were any further proof required) *both the truth of your assertions, and the reality of the dangers* to which the sovereigns, as well as the regular governments, are exposed wherever these societies are tolerated. I beg you will be convinced, sir, of the distinguished consideration with which I have the honor to be, sir, yours, &c.

VON HAMELBERG.

MINDEN, *(Westphalia) July* 27, 1800.

The preceding letters were communicated by Dr. Robison to the editors of the Anti-Jacobin Review, and from that copied in the New England Palladium, of May 29, 1801.

These letters came attended with an anecdote, which, though not supported by equal vouchers, yet so perfectly accords with the practices of the German Union, and so satisfactorily accounts for the scarcity of Robison's work in Germany, as induces me to give it a place in the conclusion of this chapter.

"Goschen, a bookseller at Leipzig, had engaged a person to make a hasty translation of Professor Robison's book, and nearly a dozen sheets had been printed, when an Englishman, who spoke German with all the purity and fluency of a native, came to his house, and telling him, that he had himself already translated the work, and that it would appear within a week, persuaded Goschen to sell him his edition, for a handsome price, which was immediately paid. By this means Goschen's translation was suppressed, and the other never appeared. The same thing, we have been assured, occurred at Berlin."

Chapter X.

The French Revolution

IF the tendency of those principles which we have seen originating in France, and communicated from thence to the German lodges, is not already apparent, we have a fair experiment before us, which fully discovers their nature. We have the fruits, to enable us to judge of the qualities of the tree. It has been observed, that the French lodges, already the nurseries of every infidel and licentious sentiment, had communicated to their German brethren those doctrines, which the wicked ingenuity of Weishaupt had wrought up into that systematical process of corruption comprised in Illuminism.

While these things were transacting in Germany, the same principles were spreading, gaining strength, and tending to an explosion in France. The French lodges had become schools, not for promoting revolutionary opinions merely, but for training men to that hardiness of iniquity, that familiarity with blood and slaughter, that erasement of every natural affection, and sentiment of tenderness, which prepare men to plunge the poignard into a brother's breast. How well these Masonic schools were adapted to prepare men for such scenes as have been exhibited in France, may be perceived from the following ceremony used in the Grand Orient.

"A candidate for reception into one of the highest

orders, after having heard many threatenings denounced against all who should betray the secrets of the order, was conducted to a place where he saw the dead bodies of several who were said to have suffered for their treachery. He then saw his own brother tied hand and foot, begging his mercy and intercession. He was informed that this person was about to suffer the punishment due for this offence, and that it was reserved for him (the candidate) to be the instrument of this just vengeance, and that this gave him an opportunity of manifesting that he was completely devoted to the order. It being observed that his countenance gave the signs of inward horror (the person in bonds imploring his mercy all the while) he was told, that in order to spare his feelings, a bandage should be put over his eyes. A dagger was then put into his right hand, and being hoodwinked, his left hand was laid on the palpitating heart of the criminal, and he was then ordered to strike. He instantly obeyed; and when the bandage was taken from his eyes, he saw that it was a lamb he had stabbed."*

Many of the French lodges needed not to be instructed in Weishaupt's theories, to qualify them for the highest degrees of Illuminism. The instructions of Voltaire had sufficiently dispossessed them of what, in the language of modern philosophy, is called *prejudice* and *superstition,* i. e. every sentiment of religious or moral obligation; but a system, and a regular subordination and correspondence, were wanting to give these principles their full force.

In this state of things, Mirabeau returned from Germany, highly illuminated; and, at his request, two of the German Areopagites, viz. Bode, and Baron de Busche, met him in France, in 1788, to form the French lodges into a duly organized body. Their business was easily transacted.

---

* Robison's Proofs, p. 299.

Before the end of March, 1789, the whole of the Grand
Orient, consisting of 266 lodges, had the secrets of Illumination communicated to them.*   By the means of secret
committees every part of this extensive body was in a state
of close connection and correspondence; and it was in the
power of the prime movers of this machine to direct the
force of the whole to any point.†

It is not, however, to be understood that every member
of this body entered into the views of the profound Illuminees.   The Duke of Orleans himself, the Grand Master of
these lodges, deceived by the conspirators with the vain
hope of ascending the throne of France, was but the tool of
their designs.

Under the direction of the German deputies, a club was
formed at Versailles, composed of the most profound
adepts, called the *Breton Club.* This society, by means of its
committees in all the illuminated lodges, obtained a most
powerful influence in the affairs of the nation. The members of this club, composed the leaders of a club, which
afterwards met at the *Covenant of Jacobins* in Paris, and
from that circumstance, was denominated the *Jacobin Club.*
The proceedings of the National Convention were entirely
subject to the influence of this usurping confederacy; and
by their secret agents, and committees they inflamed the
minds of the populace, and directed their blind rage at
pleasure.   It was the atrocious measures of these banditti
which gave to the French revolution its peculiarly horrid
features, and has attached perpetual infamy to the term
Jacobin.‡

---

* Robison's Proofs, p. 287, 303-307. Barruel's Memoirs, Vol. IV. p.
210-213.

† Ibid. p. 307; and Vol. II. p. 239.

‡ Robison's Proofs, p. 311, 376. Barruel's Memoirs, Vol. IV. Chap. 11
and 12. It is really a cause of pain to the author, that he finds himself

As a great variety of circumstances, too many to be introduced into this work, and which cannot be abridged without weakening their force, are adduced by Barruel, in proof of the influence of this illuminated society in directing the revolution; I beg leave to adduce some evidence of this fact from another quarter.

That judicious and accurate observer, John Moore, M. D. was, at the period of which we are speaking, occasionally in Paris, and frequently attended at the national assembly, and the Jacobin club, and though then ignorant of the systematical combination which guided the revolution, yet remarked, that "most questions of great importance are discussed in the Jacobin society of Paris, before they are introduced into the national assembly; and the success they are likely to have in the second, may be generally known by that which they have in the first. Societies of the same name and nature are established all over France, which hold a regular correspondence with the parent society at Paris, and by mutually communicating information and advice, act with wonderful efficacy on important occasions."

He also quotes, with approbation, a letter from M. la Fayette, of June 16, 1792, who then perceived that he had been kept ignorant of the real views of some whom he had considered as the friends of a just and equal liberty. His expressions are, "The Jacobin faction has produced all the disorders; it is that society which I loudly accuse of it. Organized like a separate empire, and blindly governed by

necessitated to introduce a term in a very odious sense, which is used to distinguish the particular political opinions of some of his countrymen, whom, whatever names they may bear, he regards as friends to religion, to order, and good government; and he now gives notice that the term *Jacobin,* as here used, is to be considered as applied, not to those who are innocently misled, but to those only who neither *fear God, nor regard man.*

some ambitious men, this society forms a distinct corpora-
tion in the middle of the French nation, whose power it
usurps, and whose representatives it subdues." This letter
proved the ruin of the Marquis.*

The American Revolution doubtless hastened the final
catastrophe of affairs in France. The French officers and
soldiers, by the new ideas which they had acquired in
America, of liberty and the rights of man, were prepared to
espouse this cause in their own country. It is obvious,
however, that the aim of the leaders in France was not to
destroy the power which oppressed the nation, but to
transfer that power into their own hands. Fayette and his
companions became the tools of their ambitious designs;
and, when they had acted the parts assigned them, were
sacrificed. Nothing was further from the views of the
French nation, at the beginning of the revolution, than what
has taken place. The object held up to them was perpetually
varying. They were first illuminated, literally blindfolded
and wheedled, till by bribes, by threatenings, and by having
their passions inflamed by false representations, they were
prepared to follow their leaders.

How different were the circumstances attending the
American revolution? Here the object in view was clear and
definite. The public will was one, and that will was faithfully executed. Accordingly, those who first stood forth the
defenders of their country's rights, acquired an influence, a
reputation, and an interest in the public confidence, which
surmounted all opposition, and which remained, unim-
paired, during the whole revolution.

The cause of this dissimilarity, in the two revolutions, is
evident. In America, the struggle was the result of a genuine spirit of freedom, seeking the protection of its rights, in

* Moore's Journal, Vol. I. p. 67-70. Boston edition, 1794.

equal laws; in France, it was the result of a faction, sacrificing to its detestable views the most sacred rights of man,
and crushing all who opposed its ambitious designs. The
friends of moderation, of justice, and a rational liberty,
when they ceased to second the views of the conspirators
were proscribed, and the illuminated chiefs, by means of the
Masonic lodges, governed the nation.

Dr. Robison, on the authority of Mr. Lefranc, President
of the seminary of the Eudists at Caen, in Normandy, and of
Mr. Latocnaye, an emigrant gentleman, represents France as
a vast Masonic combination, directed by secret influence.
In proof of this it is observed, "that all the irreligious and
seditious doctrines of the day, and the enthusiastic principles by which the public mind was, as it were, set on fire,
were the subjects of perpetual harangues in the Mason
lodges; that the distribution of France into departments,
districts, circles, cantons, &c. is perfectly similar, and with
the same denominations, to a distribution which he had
remarked in the correspondence of the Grand Orient; that
the President's hat, in the national assembly, is copied from
that of a Grand Master; that the scarf of a municipal officer
is the same with that of a brother apprentice; that when the
assembly celebrated the revolution in the cathedral, they
accepted of the highest honors of Masonry, by passing
under an *arch of steel,* formed by the drawn swords of two
ranks of brethren, and that the national assembly protected
the meetings of Free Masons, while it peremptorily prohib-
ited every other private meeting."*

It was a discovery of the horrid designs of these conductors of the French revolution, and not, as some pretend,
a dereliction of the principles of liberty, which has alienated
the virtuous part of our countrymen from their attachment

---

* Robison's Proofs, p. 294-298.

to the cause of France. When it was announced in America, that millions of Frenchmen were striving for freedom, who did not bestow a benediction on their cause, and fervently pray for its success? The triumphs of France were celebrated here with real joy, and her misfortunes were lamented as our own. Long did we strive to palliate her crimes, and long did we invent excuses for her enormities. But when at length the mask fell off, and we saw in the boasted friend of his country the disgusting atheist, the factious leader, the man who could smile at carnage, and feast on havoc and war, our feelings revolted; we could no longer receive as brethren, men who proved themselves enemies of religion, of order, of humanity.

The cooperation of the Illuminees of other nations, and their joint exertions to extend the revolution, prove that it was the work of that order; and that France was no less indebted to her secret agents than to her martial prowess, for the unexampled success of her arms.

At the commencement of the revolution, a manifesto was sent from the grand national lodge of Free Masons, (so it is entitled) at Paris, signed by the Duke of Orleans, as Grand Master, addressed to the lodges in all the respectable cities of Europe, exhorting them to unite for the support of the French revolution, and to kindle a spirit of revolution through all lands; some of these were addressed to those, of which assistance they were assured, and to such were given earnest exhortations to *establish, in every quarter, secret schools of political education; and schools for the education of children, under the direction of well disciplined masters; and offers of pecuniary assistance for this purpose, and for the encouragement of writers in favor of the revolution, and for patriotic booksellers, who suffer by their endeavors to suppress publications which have an opposite tendency.* All this is genuine Illuminism, and may help us to account for the mysterious scarcity of Dr. Robison's work in Germany.*

Among many other foreign lodges, the grand national lodge at Paris, had the particular direction of a club, in the form of a Masonic lodge, called *Propaganda,* which met weekly, and had its agents and emissaries in all parts of Europe.

These facts are collected from a Hamburg Journal, for 1790, and from a publication of Professor Hoffman, whom the Illuminees had long striven to gain to their interests, and who was employed by the more respectable Masons, to make public these machinations of the occult lodges. The result of his inquires was, "that the Propaganda works in every corner to this hour, and its emissaries run about in all the four quarters of the globe, and are to be found in numbers in every city that is a seat of government."†

These invisible agents were by no means idle or unsuccessful. There is reason to believe that France was much indebted to them for their progress in Germany, Holland, Italy, and other parts. The proofs brought in support of these facts are too much involved with circumstances to find a place here. One curious instance, however, related in a book called Paragraphen; in another performance, with the title of Cri de la Raison; and in a third, called Les Masques arrachées, must not be omitted. The instance referred to, is the following.

Custine was accused before the revolutionary tribunal of treachery, by Zimmerman, for refusing the offer of Manheim, when he himself engaged to deliver it into his hands. Custine's answer is remarkable. "Hardly," said he, "had I set foot in Germany, when this man, and all the fools

---

* See page 102.

† Robison's Proofs, p. 315-319. Barruel's Memoirs, Vol. IV. p. 283, 306.

of his country, besieged me, and would have delivered up to me their towns and villages. What occasion had I to do anything to Manheim, when the prince was neutral?"*

These secret agents of Illuminism, appear to have had another object attached to their mission, viz. the removal of those who stood much in the way of the revolution. When it was understood that Gustavus III, king of Sweden, was to command the confederate armies, Ankerstroem, by the expeditious process of assassination, relieved the Jacobins from their fears, and in recompense they honor him with a statue.†

When the expected union of the emperor of Germany and the king of Prussia, alarmed the Jacobins, the following *comfortable* reflections were annexed to the account in a Strasburgh Journal, No. 53, *"In those countries, where the fate of several millions of men, hangs on a bit of paste, or on the rupture of a little vein, one can calculate on nothing. A single indigestion, or a drop of blood forced from its proper vessels, will be sufficient to dissolve this brilliant union."* This comment on the expected union was dated from Vienna, the 26th of February, 1792. Leopold died (poisoned) on the 1st of March following.‡

On the succeeding August, it was motioned in the national assembly, "To levy a body of twelve-hundred patriotic volunteers, by a pension of two thousand livres yearly, with a reversion to their children to the third generation; whose business it should be to assassinate the generals and princes who commanded the armies which attacked France. An apprehension of reprisals prevented

* Robison's Proofs, p. 311-313. Barruel's Memoirs, Vol. IV. Chap 13.
† Barruel's Memoirs, Vol. I. p. 123.
‡ Barruel's Memoirs, Vol. IV. p. 308. Travels of two Frenchmen in the North, Vol. V. Chap. 12.

the adoption of this proposal." Mr. Moore in his account of this business, adds this circumstance, "That though it did not pass in the assembly, it was by them sent to the commission extraordinaire."*

The fate of the emperor taught his young successor more caution. His first care was to dismiss all the Italian cooks, that he might not become a victim to what was called the *Naples broth*.† The Illuminee, who believes that all means lawful for the attainment of a good end, can feel no remorse for such deeds of darkness; but, for the honor of modern times, it is desirable that our history should not be stained with many similar facts.

---

* Moore's Journal, Boston edit. 1794. Vol. I. p. 128-131.
† Barruel's Memoirs, Vol. IV. p. 308. Robison's Proofs, p. 311.

Chapter XI.

A Summary View of Illuminism

T H E S E are the leading features of that system of deception in which we see the enemies of religion quitting the open field of argument, in which they have so often been defeated, and flying to the arts of sophistry, corruption, and concealment. But it is not from a cursory glance that we can acquire a just idea of the depths of that wicked subtlety comprised in Illuminism. Let us take a view of this destructive engine in a more compact operation.

Imagine an illuminated Insinuator attacking a youth of talents and principle, in whom the moral sense of right and wrong is yet vigorous; for it is for the seduction of such, more particularly, that the artful process of Illumination is designed. From this Insinuator he hears, as by accident, however, that there are schools of wisdom, seats of science, in which the *wise* and *good* are uniting for the important end of secretly ruling mankind, and thus delivering them from those calamities, for which all other means are found to be ineffectual. If, by such suggestions, he is led to express a desire to become a member of this society, the Insinuator promises his utmost assistance; but he is told, that this is the reward only of long approved merit.

To excite his curiosity, it is intimated, that there exist doctrines solely transmitted by secret traditions, because they are above the comprehension of common minds; and letters, filled with mysterious characters, are, as it were incautiously, exposed to his view. To increase his ardor to become a member, the Insinuator expatiates frequently on the supreme pleasure of secretly reigning; and remarks that it is easy for one man of parts to lead thousands, if he but knew his own advantages. That he may be led to consider the interests of the order as his own, he is told of its readiness and power to protect him, and secure his success in all the pursuits of life. Questions of the most ensnaring nature are proposed to discover his sentiments, and books, secretly conveying the poison on infidelity, are made use of to corrupt them. If he discovers a weak part, it is noted for a point of attack. If he expresses a doubt respecting any of the important principles of religion and morality, he is sure of being applauded for his strength of mind in rising above the prejudices of education, which he is often told, are the source of all our errors. He is placed in situations were he hears the more artful sophistry used to prove, that patriotism and private affections are narrow-minded prejudices; that the bonds of marriage and parental authority are encroachments on the natural rights of man; that suicide is lawful; that sensual pleasures correspond with the law of nature, and that it is proper to employ, for a good purpose, those means which wicked men use for evil purposes.

While every art is thus employed to undermine the principles of morality and religion, his fears are lulled by constant declamations on the excellence of virtue, and the highly honorable, and most useful and benevolent intentions of the superiors of the order. It is one of the prime arts of Illuminism to extol the name of virtue, in general, and at the same time, to sap its foundation in every particular. The object is continually varying, and the mind, led by new invented systems and explanations, in a thousand different directions, is, at length, totally bewildered, and all clear distinction between truth and error is lost. How can the unwary youth escape these snares so artfully spread, and sufficient, indeed, *"if it were possible, to deceive the very elect?"*

And what could have been the design of this subtle process of deception, of all these studied phrases, and nicely adjusted degrees? Were they designed merely to discover the ingenuity of the contriver? Or, did he who contrived them, in fact, contemplate some great revolution, which rendered the introduction of all this machinery necessary? The latter is not denied by those who most zealously advocate the innocence of Illuminism. They were intended, they acknowledge, to demolish the strong holds of superstition and despotism. But when the mind is dispossessed of all that these terms imply, in the language of Illuminism, what remains? What religious principle, moral sentiment, or social affection, can exist in that heart which has been the subject of this truly diabolical renovation?

Were this question proposed to an Illuminee, his answer doubtless would be, What can exist? The noblest of all affections, the sum of all virtue, *Cosmopolitism.* Far from discarding virtue, we only are her true worshippers, who erect her temple, not on the narrow foundation of private affection, but on the broad basis of universal love.

As this term comprises everything of duty and moral obligation to which the Illuminee makes any pretensions, it becomes necessary, in order to our forming a judgment of that system, that this boasted virtue should pass a more particular examination.

A Cosmopolite, then, is a citizen of the world, or one who has banished from his breast all partial private affections. One who loves his country, his family, his friends, and benefactors, only as they are parts of the whole, and can sacrifice them without remorse, whenever he conceives it will be promotive of the general good. The adoption of this nominal, but fictitious virtue, for such it is when opposed to private duties, is an instance of art not exceeded by any of the subtleties of Illuminism. Its plausibility renders it a convenient mark for men, destitute of real good, who wish to be thought possessed of the most exalted virtue. It is a garment suited to all the forms which these modern Proteuses can wish to assume. It is a term replete with fallacy and deception, and is made to mean nothing, or anything, as the illuminated possessor pleases.

A principal of universal benevolence, or good will to being in general, doubtless enters into the composition; and, indeed, forms the foundation of all right social affections. He who loves his friend merely from this consideration, that he is his friend, has no love to him as a fellow creature, and therefore, is destitute of right social affections.* But how is this principle of universal benevolence to be expressed? In the same manner as the soldier expresses his attachment to the cause in which he is engaged, and to the army of which he is a member; by firmly maintaining his post, and faithfully executing the orders of his commander. To promote the general interests of mankind is to

---

* A late European writer on this subject observes, that "Extended benevolence is the last and most perfect *fruit* of the private affections:" but if the tree be destroyed the fruit certainly must fail. And thus, according to this theory, if all private relations, and therewith private affections are destroyed, extended, or universal benevolence cannot exist, unless there can be fruit without a tree, or an effect without a cause. See Hall's Sermon on Infidelity, page 39.

My disapprobation of this sentiment, in which I have taken the liberty to dissent from this justly celebrated writer, gives me an opportunity, which I gladly embrace, to recommend this most excellent performance, as meriting at all times, and at the present in particular, the attention of mankind.

discharge the duties of our respective stations; extending occasional aid, as opportunity offers, to our fellow creatures in distress. On the contrary, he who neglects the duties of his private sphere, serves the public as the soldier does his cause, who forsakes his post and wanders through the ranks creating disorder and confusion.

Such is the modern Cosmopolite. Having effectually eradicated all those narrow-minded prejudices which lead other men to be grateful to their friends, to provide for their families, and to serve their country, his task of social duty is at and end, unless he fancies that he is bound to labor for the general good, by forming theories, projecting revolutions, or removing the prejudices from mankind. The things last mentioned, become his duty, on his system, whenever he is pleased to fancy that they will be promotive of the general good; which justifies the assertion, that Cosmopolitism signifies nothing, or anything, as the possessor pleases.

The Cosmopolite, scorning the narrow sphere of private duties which Providence has appointed him, ascends the throne of the Supreme Ruler, and upon the great scale of universal being, judges for himself, what part belongs to him on the theater of life.

On this ground we find Weishaupt justifying his attempt to procure an abortion. He confidently pleads, that what he did in that affair, was no more than what he ought to have done to secure his character, and seems to claim no small degree of praise for doing so much to preserve the order, of which he was the founder, and which would have suffered extremely by his loss of reputation. The same principle, in his view, would justify his adepts, in plundering Masonic funds, ecclesiastical revenues, and books and writings from libraries. It was lawful, for the same reason, to destroy the reputation of such as were opposed to his order, and to make use of pious frauds to overcome men's prejudices against the doctrines of Illuminism.   Such practices, which mankind have been accustomed to reprobate, were deeds of virtue in Weishaupt's view, when done to promote the interests of an institution calculated for the advancement of human happiness.

France reasoned in the same manner.   Having established this principle, that her revolution included whatever could exalt, refine, or bless mankind, in the fullness of her Cosmopolitism, she swore eternal enmity to kings; sent forth her emissaries to promote in other nations, insurrections against the government; proffered protection and assistance to all promoters of revolutions, and even forced constitutions, framed in Paris, on those who neither desired, or would have received them but under the terrors of the bayonet.   These benevolent plans have, indeed, been productive of the most cruel exactions, robberies, and indescribable scenes of misery; but it is a narrow-minded prejudice, the French Philosopher will tell you, to compare these partial evils with the blessings of a revolution.   This, gentle reader, is *Cosmopolitism.*

It is happy that these Cosmopolites cannot communicate their principles to the brutal race, lest they, leaving their proper charge to perish, should bestow their care where it is not needed.   No; the great Author of nature, by indelible instinct, has taught them the same lesson of wisdom which he had addressed to our understandings, *"Let everyone provide for his own house."*   It is happier still that they have not been able to transmit their universal benevolence to other worlds, and to persuade the great luminary of our system to wander from his orbit, leaving us to frost and darkness, to revolutionize other systems.   No; every creature, which has not rebelled against the first great law of order, promotes the general good, by abiding in its prescribed sphere of action. Wherever this law is transgressed ruin and misery will be the consequence.

This is the evidence on which we are to form our judgment of the nature and tendency of Illuminism; and what do we see, but a destructive combination against the most precious interests of mankind? It appears, that the real nature and tendency of Illuminism is to be found, by precisely reversing its ostensible aim, and the pretended object of its advocates.

By universal citizenship and disinterested love, the Illuminee intends the destruction of all whom he cannot render the dupes of his designs. Morality, with him, means the unbounded indulgence of every corrupt bias of human nature, only preserving such an exterior as shall better enable him to impose on mankind. The glorious emancipation from slavery, to which he invites men, consists in the blind subjugation of all their actions to the unknown superiors of the order. His humanity is the extinction of every tie of nature, of every social affection; even marriage is, in the view of the Illuminee, an insufferable monopoly, and every check to a brutal indulgence of the sexual affections, a species of tyranny. His philosophy consists of theories contradicted by universal experience. His religion is atheism dressed to the taste of the scrupulous conscience. His useful and important discoveries, are new means of assassination, abortion, and peculation. His Creator is chance; and his future glorious hope, everlasting sleep.

The original source of Illuminism, and the principle which, in a greater or less degree, influences all who are actuated by its genuine spirit, doubtless, is an innate enmity to Christianity, and a desire to be free from the checks which its holy doctrines oppose to the corruptions of the heart.

Motives different from this have, however, united their

operation in extending this combination, especially in its hostility to social order, and an energetic government. Men who wish to possess property for which they have not labored, and men of property who want power, these, and men who never enjoy themselves but in a storm, and whose revolutionary minds could not rest even in the calm of Paradise; all of this description, find their several ends promoted by disturbing the peace of society, removing the ancient landmarks, overturning useful establishments, and breaking down the barriers which have secured the rights and property of mankind.

For effecting these designs, Illuminism furnishes a most artful and systematic process. It supplies the want of power, by subtle insinuations. It teaches to bind men with invisible bands; to govern them by their prejudices and passions, and to delude them by a false light, perpetually varying the object of pursuit, until the mind is lost in endless wanderings, and deprived of every permanent principle of action.

Another observable trait in the character of these deceivers is, their pretended attachment to the cause they secretly endeavor to undermine. Judging from their declarations, they appear the firm friends of government and religion, at the same time that they are plying every secret art to effect their destruction. These "pious frauds must indeed be explained away," but this is easily done among those to whom they have communicated the spirit of the order.

Chapter XII.

Objections Considered

I am sensible that great efforts have been made, both in Europe and America, to convince mankind of the harmless nature of Illuminism, and that its operation, whatever its tendency was, has long since ceased. But the wonderful zeal and bitterness, which have been exhibited on this subject, instead of abating, justly increase suspicion. If my neighbor fancies himself beset by ghosts and hobgoblins, I may well pity him, and endeavor to remove the painful illusion; but is there any cause for bitter resentment? Shall I be at the pains of inventing, and circulating falsehoods to convince mankind that my neighbor's fears are imaginary? That falsehoods of the grossest nature have been most industriously propagated, and vengeance of the most horrid kind denounced against those who have expressed their apprehensions of the destructive effects of Illuminism, are facts. But why is thus, if Illuminism is that silly, harmless tale which by some it is represented to be? Or why was not Robison's work to be found in Germany? This is not the way to remove jealousies. Where there is such a fluttering and outcry, we naturally conclude that some are deeply wounded.

The peculiar invisibility of this order must greatly invalidate the most positive declarations in its favor, however honestly intended. Admitting the Mr. Ebeling, in particular, is, as he asserts, neither an Illuminee nor a Mason, and that his declarations on this subject are the result of conviction, must this be admitted as conclusive evidence? A similar declaration has been made by many, in the uprightness of their hearts, who have been admitted even to the threshold of the mysteries; for they have all along had the most positive assurances, that the object of the order was the advancement of civil and religious liberty, in their most perfect degrees.

Did those adepts, who retained their respect for the scriptures, believe that they were supporting a system of Spinozism? Or did initiated princes believe that they were protecting an order which was aiming to reduce them to the rank of plebeians? Yet persons of each of the above descriptions gave their warm support to this Anti-Christian, disorganizing confederacy. Is then the judgment of professor Ebeling to be deemed infallible?

From the peculiar nature of the subject, it is obvious, that witnesses of the highest credibility in other matters, cannot be depended on in this; here is so much collusion, art, and studied concealment, that nothing but stubborn facts, their own writings, and secret, confidential communications, can be reasonably admitted to be of weight in determining the views of the order.

If Mr. Ebeling's proximity to the scene of action, afforded him some special advantages for estimating circumstantial evidence, is he not likewise exposed, from this situation, to some peculiar disadvantages? Doubtless he had frequent, and most positive assurances from many worthy and good men, men as deserving in character, at least, as Weishaupt, of whom he speaks so respectfully, that Illuminism was perfectly harmless, and even highly beneficial to mankind. Is it not very possible that such declarations, made with the subtle sophistry, and plausibility in which Illuminism so much abounds, should bias the judgment of the charitable professor? Then, in proportion to his nearness of the suggested, but undiscovered, danger, he would naturally become confident that it did not exist. It certainly adds importance to these observations, that others, who had at least equal advantages with Mr. Ebeling to judge of the real views of these conspirators, yet differed much from him in opinion.

But can these things be real? Can human nature be so debased, so lost to every principle, not of religion only, but of social virtue? Or could any person, capable of inventing such a system, imagine that it was practicable, and that any considerable number of mankind would submit to such abominable impositions? These reflections, I confess, are, to this moment, pressing on my mind, and raise a momentary doubt, which nothing but the most clear and indubitable evidence can remove. But this doubt, we find upon reflection, arises more from the novelty of the subject, than from anything in it that is really incredible. Is not all wickedness, madness and folly? Is not the want of opportunity and abilities, the real cause why mankind do not exhibit more frequent instances of mischievous madness? Does the history of past ages leave us room to wonder at any act of extravagance, which is credibly attested, because it is in the highest degree unreasonable, and destructive, both to the perpetrator and his fellow creatures? If revelation has not sufficiently taught us *what is in man,* the French revolution may surely convince us, that there is no species or degree of wickedness, within the compass of human ability, which is beyond the corruption of the human heart. Every impious, immoral, cruel, and disorganizing sentiment, ever taught in the school of Spartacus, has been exemplified in late transactions which have taken place in Europe.

It is not, indeed, to be supposed that all the proceedings of the society were minutely conformable to the adopted system: we know they were not. The machine was too unwieldy to be applied in all cases. The heads of the order reserved a right of deviating according to their judgment of circumstances. Some needed not Weishaupt's process of seduction, to prepare them for the highest mysteries of Illuminism. A complete system may be useful as a general directory, even when it is not brought into universal operation. In this instance the vanity of the author, doubtless excited him to render his work perfect, and connected in all its parts. The objection which some make to the existence of Illuminism, that it is too complicated and cumbersome ever to obtain the object ascribed to the projector, cannot be important.

While the Illuminees complain of great severity in the proceedings of the government against their order, others, judging of the degree of the crime by the punishment, conclude, from the lightness of the latter, that the former could not be equal to what has been represented. Deprivation of office, imprisonment, and some instance of banishment, appear indeed to have been punishments inadequate to such atrocious conspiracies. Weishaupt himself expected nothing short of the gallows in case of his detection. That his expectations were not realized, was, doubtless, owing in part, to the secret influence of Illuminism over the measures of government; and still more, to the many respectable characters to be found to be partially involved, which rendered it expedient that the subject should be treated with all possible lenity.

In addition to this, it is to be observed, that the weakness and inferiority of many of the German principalities, reduce them to the necessity of accommodating the measures of government to particular circumstances. On the authority of private letters from Germany, Barruel relates, That the Duke of Brunswick, in particular, justified his not proceeding to extremities with the Illuminees in his states, by saying, "Supposing I should send them away, they would only go elsewhere and calumniate me;" adding, "a league ought to be entered into by the German princes, to suffer them in no part of the Empire."*

* Barruel's Memoirs, Vol. IV. p. 317.

Chapter XIII.

Collateral Proofs, and General Observations, in relation to Europe

T H E evidence, and authentic documents, which have been exhibited, it is conceived are such, as can leave no doubt of the existence and active operation of Illuminism from 1776, until these works of darkness were brought to light, and their promoters compelled to change their mode of procedure. Most of the late European writers, where propriety would permit, allude to it as an indubitable fact. It is not, indeed, denied even by those who seem most disposed to quiet our apprehensions on this subject: their efforts are directed to prove, either that its operation is now at an end, or, that it never was designed to produce, nor, was indeed capable of producing, the evils ascribed to it. Whether the subversion of superstition and despotism was the whole aim of these plotting geniuses, their writing and conduct will enable us to judge.

The statements and observations in this chapter are principally designed to show, that the contagious poison is still spreading and infecting society, threatening the destruction of everything important to mankind, and therefore, that the history of this sect is a subject highly interesting.

Admitting that the order of the Illuminees is now extinct, their systems and doctrines remain; the books by which they communicated their poison are in circulation; the arts by which they inveigled and corrupted the minds of men are not forgotten, and the former members of this society still possess the skill, the wicked subtlety, to which the care of Weishaupt formed his adepts. To prove that such destructive arts have existed, is virtually to prove that they still exist; that is, that the care and caution of the wise and good ought to be the same, as if they were assured of their present existence and actual operation. Can it be a doubt whether wicked men will use the most effectual weapons in their power? Whether they will adopt those means which they judge best calculated to promote their purposes? It belongs to the art of fortification to provide against every possible mode of attack. The invention of artillery pointed out the necessity of new means of defense, and it became the engineer to construct works, which would repel their destructive violence. The legislator, the instructor of youth, the moralist, the defender of Christianity, have new arts to encounter, new modes of attack and instruments of mischief to guard against; how necessary, then, that they should become acquainted with the weapons of their enemies, and of their new modes of attack?

Although the dissolution of this combination has been confidently asserted, the evidence of the fact does not appear. The interruption it has received from detection, would naturally produce an increase of caution; but can it be supposed to effect any change in the wishes or designs of the conspirators? Is the thing in itself probable? The proof adduced is merely of the negative kind, and much of this is contradicted by plain facts.

In 1794, it was announced to the public, that from 1790, "every concern of the Illuminees has ceased." But in addition to what has been already related of a contrary aspect, many circumstances contradict this assertion.

In 1791, a spark of Illuminism caught in Ireland, and spread with astonishing rapidity, threatening a universal conflagration. The conspirators there assumed the denomination of United Irishmen.* This extensive combination was concealed under forms very similar to those of Masonry, and the whole was methodized upon the graduated scale of Illuminism.

The subordinate societies consisted of thirty members, and were under the direction of a Baronial committee, composed of a delegate from each society within the Barony. The Baronial committees in each county, in like manner, elected delegates, who formed a county committee. Delegates from each county committee, formed, in like manner, a provincial committee for the government and direction of the several county committees, in each of the four provinces; and these provincial directories appointed the general executive, whose residence was in the metropolis.

The secretaries of each of these committees, were to be taken from an higher committee, and by them the whole correspondence was maintained, and the orders of the

---

* See the report of the Committee of Secrecy, presented to the Irish House of Commons, July, 1797, with the papers and testimonies upon which said report was founded: 2nd edition London, 1798, for John Stockdale; and the Speech of the Lord Chancellor, Feb. 19, 1798, reprinted for J. Stockdale.

What is here introduced in relation to Ireland, is not designed to intimate that the people of that country did not need a redress of grievances. It is noticed merely as evidence of the existence of Illuminism. It originated from foreign influence. The system adopted was perfectly in the style of the new order. The passions of the people were inflamed, and their judgment blinded by misrepresentations. They were deceived as to the real object of their leaders. By the same means insurrections may be excited under any government where the people are in a similar state of vice and ignorance.

executive transmitted through the different degrees. These orders, for the greater security, were, if possible, to be communicated verbally, or otherwise, to be immediately destroyed.

One object of the union specified in the constitution was, that of communicating with similar societies in other parts, and particularly with the Jacobin club in Paris. In addition to the usual oaths of secrecy, submission, &c. every member was solemnly sworn never to give evidence against a brother, in any court of justice, *whatever might be his crime*. Another requisite oath was *fidelity to the French republic*.*

In April, 1796, the outline of a treaty with France was drawn up by the general committee of the union, and transmitted to the French directory, in consequence of which a French force made its appearance at Bantry Bay, on the 24th December, but by a mistake between the parties, with respect to the time agreed upon for the invasion, the Insurgents were not prepared to cooperate, and the expedition failed. The accounts detailed in the reports of the several committees, represent the numbers of this association to be vastly numerous. It is particularly stated, that 150,000 were organized and enrolled in the province of Ulster.†

Similar societies, in close union and correspondence with this, were formed in England, and Scotland, under different names, but pursuing the same object.

A statement, still more interesting to Americans, is found in the report of a provincial meetings, dated Randolstown, August 14, 1797, from which it appears, that a number of societies were formed in *North America,* from

---

* Chancellor's Speech, p. 32 – Irish report, Appendix, No. 4.
† Appendix, No. 31.

which, in the last eight days, *two hundred and eleven dollars* had been received.*

The ostensible object of this union, was a parliamentary reform; but the correspondence with the directory, and the testimony of several witnesses, afforded abundant proof, that this was held up merely to blind the people, and that the real object of the *chiefs* was, a revolution, of which the French revolution was to be the model.

Barruel relates several instances in which the adepts were found fomenting conspiracies against the government, both in Austria and Prussia, long after the cessation of all the operations of Illuminism were announced to the public. These attempts were truly formidable, and were rendered abortive, only by those strange accidental occurrences, by which a governing Providence disappoints the devices of the crafty. One instance is worthy of notice, as a curiosity. Mehalovich, formerly a capuchin, was a principal in a conspiracy in Germany. While he was out one day, a domestic, playing with one of his fellow servants, for the sake of humor, put on the capuchin habit, which his master had preserved among his clothes, when his master unexpectedly returned. The servant, in order to prevent being discovered, hid himself under the bed. Mehalovich, with two other conspirators, entered the room; and thinking themselves secure, they conversed, unreservedly, upon the conspiracy, which was to break out in three days. Mehalovich took five hundred thousand florins, which were hidden in a harpsichord, and gave them to one of the conspirators for execution of the plan. After they had left the room, the servant went immediately and discovered the whole plot to the ministers of state. In the result, Mehalovich, with eight accomplices, was executed, and many

* Appendix, No. 14.

others were condemned to exile, or to perpetual imprison-ment.

This conspiracy exhibits a remarkable instance of the means by which modern revolutions have been effected. The party, desirous of a new order of things, through their influence at court, found means of forming a garrison at Vienna, of substantial and honest citizens, little accustomed to bear arms. These new raised corps, they treated with the greatest severity, under the pretense, that what they did was by order of the emperor; hoping by this to render the government obnoxious to them.*

Habitually viewing Europeans as deprived of the rights of men, and groaning under oppression, our attention has been naturally diverted from considering the real character of modern revolutionists, and the tendency of their meas-ures and principles. From the happy success of their own revolution, Americans, in particular, have incautiously indulged the idea, that a revolution must meliorate society; that nothing more is necessary to render men free, prosper-ous, and happy, than to overturn ancient establishments. Even under the administrations of WASHINGTON and ADAMS, these children of change, fancied a revolution necessary to preserve our liberties. But what has been exhibited in Europe, may teach us that it is time to pause, and consider consequences.

Would the deluded people of Ireland probably have improved their situation by overturning their own govern-ment, and throwing themselves into the arms of France? What recompense has France herself found for her slaugh-ter of millions, her exhausted treasuries, and the scenes of indescribable distress which have attended her revolution? Can a people enjoy, or preserve the blessings of temperate

---

* Barruel's Memoirs, Vol. IV. p. 311, 312.

liberty, until they are enlightened and virtuous? Will unprincipled, ambitious men exert the influence they gain over mankind, to make them free or happy? Have none but tyrants reason to dread this new, revolutionizing spirit? Was not Switzerland free? Were the magistrates of Geneva despots? In fine, is that revolutionary power, which consists in blinding its agents and inflaming the bad passions of a nation by false representations, desirable in any government?

If opposition to constituted authorities, and a pretended zeal for the rights of men, are proofs of patriotism and benevolence, the present may well be called *the golden age;* but we have been sufficiently entertained with vague declamations, it is time to attend to facts and experience.

It is obvious that society cannot subsist, unless those are governed who will not govern themselves. Were all the members of a community invariably disposed to practice righteousness, to such a community, a government of restraint would be unnecessary. On the contrary, a society composed of men of an opposite character, needs the strong hand of power to preserve the public tranquillity. Such a government tends indeed to abuse, and perhaps there may not be an instance, where this rigorous exercise of authority is maintained, with a perfect regard to justice and the rights of the subject. It is to be regretted that men, invested with power, are so little disposed to approve themselves the fathers and benefactors of their subjects. But is it therefore desirable, in the present state of mankind, that every government should be revolutionized into a republic? Is the modern, fashionable oath, of "hatred to all kings," dictated by an enlightened and Christian benevolence? That man might as reasonably lay claim to benevolence, who should loose the hands of a mad-man, and set him at liberty to destroy his family and himself. Until a people are enlightened and virtuous, republican freedom will degenerate into licentiousness, and afford an opportunity to the factious and ambitions, by enflaming the passions of men, to erect a tyranny more to be dreaded than that of the most arbitrary despot on earth.

No nation in modern Europe has suffered more from an unlimited monarchy that France; but, separate from all the mischiefs which her mad politics have produced to other parts of the world, there certainly has been no equal period under her most despotic kings, productive of evils, to be compared with those which have attended the late revolution; and these evils must probably have continued, if general BONAPARTE had not fortunately acquired such unlimited control over the nation, as has restored order and peace.

It is futile to attempt to avoid the conclusion, which this fact affords, by observing, that these evils are to be imputed, not to the people of France, but to factious leaders, who have made them the dupes of their ambitious views; for it is the wretched ignorance, and depravity of a people which make the dupes of such leaders. How gross must be the ignorance of a people who can believe, that such men as Danton, Marat, and Robespierre, are friends to real liberty, and the rights of man? A vitiated society will always have such leaders. We may safely estimate the characters of a people, by that of the persons in whom they place confidence. This consideration alone, proves, that virtue and information are necessary to the support of a free government. Where these are wanting, persons of the above description will never fail, by the cry of tyranny, and a pretended zeal for equal rights, to increase the jealousy of a people against rules of their own choice; to withdraw from them the necessary confidence, and to transfer that confidence, most improperly indeed, to themselves. To this evil, republican governments, from the lenity and indulgence which enters into their constitution, have always been particularly exposed; but the danger is greatly augmented since the arts of deception have been wrought into a system, and the active *Propaganda* of Illuminism has been laboring to undermine every government within reach of its influence. From this cause, every considerable republic in Europe has undergone a revolution; and the preservation of governments of a more rigorous form, is owning to their greater energy in repelling the invading enemy.

The American revolution took place under the happiest of omens. It did not originate from the blinding influence of designing men; it was not excited by the ambitious desire of rendering America mistress of the world; but it owed its rise and progress to a just sense, in the Americans, of the rights of men, of what was due to themselves, and to posterity, and a wise, patriotic, and virtuous determination to resist the first encroachments of arbitrary power. Simplicity of manners, habits of economy, industry, and moderation, together with ample means of information, of moral and religious instruction, every circumstance seemed to promise permanency to our government, and a rich harvest of the blessings of freedom. Never was the experiment of a republican government made with fairer prospects of success. Yet, even here has anarchy reared her horrid front, and struck terror into the hearts of Americans. The arts of intrigue have withdrawn public confidence from approved worth, and tried merit, and all the energies of government have been called into action to suppress a spirit of insurrection, and open opposition to constitutional measures.

There yet appears a large number of citizens, we hope a great majority, who seem sensible to the importance of electing men of principle, and of supporting the moral, and religious institutions of our country; and while such is our situation, we are not to despair of the republic.

It is far from the design of these observations, to prove, that a republican government is either undesirable, or impracticable; they are intended merely to exhibit the absurdity of the idea, which many have adopted, that nothing more is necessary to make any people happy than to reject their own government, and receive a constitution from France. Whatever may be the result of the experiment now making in America, the events which have taken place here, as well as in Europe, give weight to the opinion, that mankind are not generally prepared for the enjoyment of republican blessings.

But it is not merely by exciting revolutions and conspiracies, that Illuminism has discovered itself in Europe, since we were told, "that all the concerns of Illuminism had ceased."

So late as February, 1798, the magistrates of Jena were compelled to punish a number of the students of that university, who had formed an association, by the name of Amicists, under the direction of some Illuminee. They had been taught to consider the oath of their association as superceding all others, even the most sacred engagement that could be made. The form of this society was Masonic; and by their secretary, they maintained a regular correspondence with other lodges. Their code taught them to consider themselves as a state within a state; enjoined the most profound secrecy, and expressly required, that, should several of them afterwards reside in the same town, they should establish a lodge, and do all in their power to propagate the society.*

On the authority of some private communications from

---

* See Minutes of the Judgment of Hamburg, No. 45. March 13.

Germany, the historian further states, that the university at Halle, was in a similar situation with that at Jena. That public insults were offered by the students, to the ministers of religion, while attending the duties of their office; that dogs were set at them while preaching, and that indecencies took place in the churches, which would not be suffered in the streets.*

The very respectable writer before quoted, of Upper Saxony, says, "In the great universities of Germany, which I have seen, or of which I have had any information, the students have the appearance of a set of rude and insolent Jacobins. In some universities, where the students amount to about a thousand or twelve-hundred, they are all formed into private societies; and that, in all the German universities, the chief study is the new system of philosophy, by which the mind is totally bewildered, and at length deprived of every solid principle of religion, morality, or sound politics. Unfortunately," he adds, "the clergy, and many, even of those who serve the country parishes, have had their minds bewildered with the metaphysical jargon of the universities. They have come to doubt, and some to deny, the truths of Christianity itself; and to assert, that it is a vulgar superstition, adapted only to the ignorant. The Old testament has very generally lost its authority; and a country clergyman, lately in company with a friend of mine, laughed heartily at the ignorance and confined notions of the clergy of the church of England, when he heard they still believe the Mosaic history of the fall of man."†

A gentleman of great respectability in Europe, in a letter to his correspondent in America, dated September, 1800, says, "I lament exceedingly, the too plain state of the public

---

* Barruel's Memoirs, Vol. IV. p. 306-316.
† Appendix to Anti-Jacobin Review, Vol. VI. p. 569.

mind on the great points of religion and morality. Religion has been so freely dealt with now in Germany, that it no longer makes the impression of former times, always mixed with some tincture of veneration. It is now entered upon with the same coolness and ease as any other matter of scientific discussion. This of itself is a misfortune. It was surely of advantage to us, that the mind could not engage in any religious research, without somewhat of the same reserve (call it superstition if you will) that one feels when discussing a point of filial duty or relation. Religion having thus lost all its use, it has even ceased to occupy its former share of room in the German Catalogues; and the scribblers have fairly begun to treat the plain *moral* duties with the same freedom. I received lately, a small performance, by one Emmering, at Frankfort, who, even under the tyranny of Custine, in 1792, had the boldness to attack the profligate speeches of Bohmer and Forster, in the Convention of Mentz. He still preserves the same unsubdued spirit; and though a layman, (a Wine merchant) he nobly maintains the cause of religion and virtue. In this little performance he mentions several most profligate publications, in which the fidelity of the husband, to the marriage bed, is systematically shown to be a frivolous prudery; and therefore, concubinage, or polygamy, perfectly proper, under certain regulations, purely civil; and, which is most lamentable, the proper courts, before which this was brought by Emmering himself, refused to take it up as a public offence. This, at Frankfort, grieved me; for during the revolution at Mentz, the inhabitants of Frankfort, behaved in a manner that is not exceeded by anything on record.

"I was the more affected by this, because I have found that Knigge and Weishaupt, after having formed very high expectations from their operations if Edessa, were disappointed; and, in 1782, reprobate Edessa in the most rancorous terms.   Philo says, 'the inhabitants are too rich, too republican, and will not be led about by the nose.'

"Emmering mentions another publication by one Semler, professedly written to weaken the parental tie, laying it down as a principle, that a man's children have only an artificial title to his fortune, unless they have aided him in the acquisition of it.   But the state, by giving that protection by which the fruits of his industry are secured to him, has a preferable and natural claim.   The aim of this unnatural principle is too barefaced, I think, to be dangerous.   But a companion to it by George Forster, is more atrocious.   The sons and daughters are made the judges of their parent's character and conduct, and if they find either *incivic,* they are peculiarly bound to denounce them as undutiful to them (their children) by giving them pernicious principles and education.   I mention these things to show how the profligate monsters have attempted to revolutionize *the mind of man.*"

We have many unequivocal proofs that this is a just representation of the state of religion and literature in Germany.   To what views and motives shall we then attribute the conduct of those gentlemen, who endeavor to compel us, by illiberal reproaches, to believe their unsupported declarations?   Do they not know that the mind naturally revolts against such unreasonable violence, such tyrannical attempts to hoodwink our understandings?

Chapter XIV.

Collateral Proofs, and General Observations, relating to the United States

THOSE who assure us that Illuminism was always harmless, and has long since been extinct in Europe, at the same time ridicule the idea of its having ever existed in America, or had any influence on our civil or religious interests. From the peculiar secrecy of the sect, these gentlemen came forward with the greatest advantages for gaining credit; for, they confidently ask, where are these Illuminees? Point them out to us. With the same confidence they assert that we were ignorant of the name of this order until it was communicated by Robison. This is true, but if they are impartial, Why do they not lay open the whole truth? Why do they not tell us that the strength of the order lies principally in concealment, and that it assumes any name or form, rather than its own proper one? Why do they not tell us, what they very well know, that, even in their native soil, Bavaria, their name and existence were equally unknown, till their deeds discovered their retreat, and induced an inquiry, which brought to light their hidden works of darkness? The inquiry before us does not respect names and appellations. We are not contending that there are, or have been, men in America, known as Illuminees. The important fact is, that men in America, under the direction and influence of a foreign head, are, or at least have been, combined in opposition to our peace, prosperity, and welfare. A rash, unfounded suggestion of this nature would be highly criminal; it is here made with solemnity, and under a conviction, that the evidence by which it is supported, affords just cause of alarm.

Upon the list of illuminated lodges, furnished by Dr. Robison, several are mentioned as existing in America before 1786.*

The zeal with which Dr. Morse has investigated this matter, as it respects this country, though it has loaded him with that kind of obloquy which is the good man's praise, has furnished some important documents with which we shall enrich this part of the subject.

In an Appendix to his Fast Sermon, of May 9, 1798, he gives us a particular account of the lodge WISDOM, instituted at Portsmouth in Virginia, as early as 1786, a branch of the Grand Orient of France, and numbered the 2660th descendant of that stock.† From an original letter, for the authenticity of which he pledges himself to the public, he has furnished us with an official list of the numbers, names, ages, places of nativity, and professions of the officers and members of this lodge, together with their horrid seal, in which, with some of the usual Masonic symbols, are interwoven emblems of carnage and death. The members of this lodge, consisting of one hundred, were chiefly emigrants from France and St. Domingo. This lodge had a deputy residing with the mother society in France, to communicate all needful instructions. Two similar societies had originated from the Portsmouth lodge, one in Virginia, the other at St. Domingo.

By the same means he had evidence of the existence of a

---

* Robison's Proofs, p. 159.

† Particular mention is made of this lodge by Barruel, Vol. IV. p. 213.

similar society at New York, called "The Grand Orient of New York," derived, in like manner, from the lodge of the same name in France. From this New York lodge issued a French lodge, called the UNION, which was the 14th branch from this secondary stock. The particular location of the other lodges, or whether the number here specified, included the whole which were then in America, were not known.

It is an important item of information, which the Doctor further communicates on this subject, that the best informed Free Masons among us, disclaim these societies; the titles of some of their dignitaries, their seal and motto they declare are not Masonic. In the close he introduces the following calculation, which, though obvious, is interesting. Admitting all these American lodges, individually, to contain an equal number of members with the lodge Wisdom, the calculation gives at that time, no less than 1700 agents of Illuminism in America, in close connection and correspondence with each other, and with the Grand Orient at Paris, from which they received constant *illumination;* and we may add, acting under the influence of a society, which was the active soul and vital spring of those scenes of horror exhibited in France and other parts of Europe.

A very respectable Mason, formerly Grand Master of all the lodges in the State in which he resided, informed me, that a letter, designed for one of the abovementioned lodges, fell into his hands while he was Grand Master, by a very natural mistake, and which left him no room to doubt the accuracy and authenticity of what Dr. Morse has stated on this subject. He could not ascertain particulars, as the time of his receiving the letter was previous to the discovery of Illuminism, and consequently it appeared more enigmatical than it probably would at present; and since that time, it has been mislaid, or taken out of his possession.

The following facts, received from unquestionable authority, confirm the truth and accuracy of the above representation. A gentlemen of high respectability, who says, "he belonged to a lodge of the *ancient* order of Masons," and was in a situation to know perfectly the character and conduct of the Portsmouth lodge, under date of March 23, 1800, writes thus to Dr. Morse; "The lodge in Portsmouth, to which you allude, in your appendix, called the French lodge, was considered by me as under the *modern term of Masonry.* Its members, in 1789, were mostly French. Some men who were respectable, and attached to our government, Dickson and Cox, particularly, belonged to the lodge at that time. It is probably about the time Admiral Cambis' fleet arrived there from St. Domingo, there might have been many enthusiastic Frenchmen admitted, which swell the number in your list."

April 11, 1800, the same gentleman writes, "That you had the good grounds to suspect the designs of the French lodge at Portsmouth in Virginia, I have no reasons, nor ever had, to doubt; and, at a time, it is evident to me, that their work was to effect the plans of France in this country; and that the bulk of the members who composed the lodge in 1797, were ready to further any designs which the French government may have had on this country, and to give their aid to carry them into effect, as they were mostly Frenchmen. The few Americans admitted were *to prevent their being suspected,* and they could operate without them; as I am convinced they never were admitted to the highest degrees."

Add to the above, that this French lodge at Portsmouth, was not in fellowship with the other lodges of the *ancient* order of Masons; and that one of its members from Germany, at a period when Americans generally thought favorably of the French revolution, declared, (and the declaration can be substantiated) that he belonged to a

lodge in Germany, in which that revolution was planned.
These facts, and those originally stated, together with
credible information, received direct from the most respectable men in Portsmouth, prove incontestably the correctness of the account which has been published of this lodge.

Although the above documents have never been con-
fronted with any evidence, unless clamor and abuse may be
so called, yet, as this mode of reasoning has its influence
with some people, I must beg leave to introduce another
respectable Masonic testimony. It is an extract, furnished
by a friend, from a printed oration, delivered February 3rd,
A. L. 5801, before the Grand Royal Arch Chapter for the
state of New York, by the Rev. John F. Ernst, Grand Chaplin.
The friend who furnishes the extract, writes that he (the
orator) "is held in high, very high estimation by the Masons
in those parts." The orator, guarding his brethren against
the wrong use which he acknowledges has been made of
Masonry, in many instances, introduces the following
sentence.

"The unravelled and deep designs of *modern* Masons,
called the Illuminati, who have almost inundated Europe,
and are gaining ground fastest in America, have clearly
demonstrated the abuse, *untyled Mason lodges have met
with;* and how they, when not presided over, and guarded by
men of knowledge, and genuine Masonic principles, *can* be
overthrown, revolutionized, and *molded according to
pleasure.*"

Are these documents deserving no credit? Shall we
renounce our reason, because some men will not believe
unless they have a sign from heaven? And if true, do they
not afford just cause of alarm? Admitting this was a full
discovery of the extent of Illuminism in America, at that
time, and that since that time, it has received no increase,
which is far from being probable; is a body of seventeen-
hundred men, acting with the force of secret societies, and

under the direction of a foreign power, compatible with the peace, quiet, and safety of this country? We need no longer wonder at the confidence the French Directory expressed in the *diplomatic skill* and influence in America, or the prevalence of the new philosophy, and the alarming change which has taken place here, in the state of religion and morals. It is no longer surprising, that every method has been adopted to excite opposition to the measures of the late administration of our government, to vilify our best characters, and to alienate the minds of the citizens from their rulers; or, that native Americans have been compelled to yield their seats to foreigners. This affords an easy explanation, of what, without this key, must appear mysterious, that a period, in which we have enjoyed all that men can enjoy of blessings of a free and excellent government, attended with a degree of prosperity, which has scarce its parallel in the history of mankind, has been a period of complaint, of tumult and insurrection. Nor is it unaccountable that we should hear it asserted, with the highest effrontery, that out greatest danger arises, not from France, from Illuminism, or self-created societies, but, from the tyranny of the clergy, and from British influence. These are among the known arts of Illuminism. Whoever has carefully observed its progress in Europe, will easily discern the features of the monster, under all its concealments. It is an axiom in Illuminism, upon which its disciples, both in Europe and America, have formed their practice, that the most egregious and absurd falsehoods, if told with confidence, and confidently repeated, will at length gain credit and influence.

As has been stated, we have ample proof, that societies have existed in America, derived from the Grand Orient in France, and intimately connected with that directing head of all the improved, or illuminated lodges in France. This evidence, coming from different quarters and distinct sources, is greatly corroborated by that circumstance, and acquires an additional claim to our belief. But will it be said, because illuminated societies, connected with those of France, once existed in America, it is not therefore certain that they were united in design with the parent society, or wished to extend the empire of Illuminism? Though Jacobin clubs were suddenly formed in every part of the United States, similar to those in France, by means of which, the Jacobins governed the nation at their pleasure, yet this, it may with as much truth be said, is no demonstration that the clubs in America were formed for the like purpose. Thus men reason, who are determined not to admit conviction. But can any person, not blinded by prejudice, doubt whence arose the opposition made to the adoption of the federal constitution, and to every measure, calculated to establish the independence, prosperity, and respectability of our country? It is not commonly to be expected, that we should be able to substantiate, by legal evidence, the secret machinations of the emissaries of darkness. Their intentions are not to be discovered by their professions, and ostensible character; but often they unwarily expose themselves to the wakeful eye of wisdom.

Before the systematical arrangements of Illuminism became public, the active interference of France in America was visible to every person of discernment, who was not opposed to conviction. It is well known that the activity of Genet, by granting commissions to privateers, procuring the enlistment of soldiers, forming clubs, extending the influence of France, and by his attempts to excite opposition to government, and to alienate the minds of the people from their rulers, produced a remonstrance on the subject from our watchful President, which rendered his recall unavoidable. To exculpate those under whose commission Genet acted, his conduct in America has been attributed to his imprudently exceeding his commission. This is easily said, as many other things have been, without a coloring of truth. Genet had his recommendation for the American appointment, in the proofs he had given of his disorganizing qualities at Geneva, where he had been the successful agent of the same detestable policy. But we are not left to conjectures respecting the grounds of his appointment. Robespierre, wishing to crush the Brissotine faction, that he might posses their power and influence, charges them with their unjust attempts against other governments, and with respect to America, says expressly, "Genet, their agent in Philadelphia, made himself chief of a club there, and never ceased to make and excite motions equally injurious and perplexing to the government."

Defeated in this attempt, by the vigilance of WASH-INGTON, but not discouraged, rendered more cautious, but not the less malicious, the agents of France still pursued, though with greater secrecy, their disorganizing system. In 1795, Fauchet's intercepted letter again disclosed their dark designs and the real character of "the pretended patriots of America." The memorable sentence, relating to the insurgents in the western counties, will not be soon forgotten. He informs his government, that the western people, "Republican by principle, independent by character and situation, they could not but accede with enthusiasm to the criminations which we have sketched."* The grievances of these deluded people, or their criminations of government, were not, it appears, suggested by their own feelings, but by *French agents,* who dictated to them what were the censurable proceedings of their constituted authorities.

This is not the first time this officious nation has sketched grievances, and excited those who were at rest, to arm themselves against their own governments. But lest

---

* Fauchet's Letter, 10th paragraph.

this *sketch* should not meet the feelings, and obtain the full approbation of these republicans, Fauchet administers to his employers, this further consolation, that "these complaints were systematizing by the conversation of *influential men,* who retired into those wild countries, and who, from principle, or by a *series of particular heart-burnings,* animated discontents, already too near to effervescence."* It must now be left with the reader to determine, whether or not he will allow Mr. Fauchet, and his influential coadjutors, the praise he claims of exciting an insurrection, which cost the United States more than a *million of dollars.*

As Mr. Fauchet has not told us what arguments his influential agents would use to promote the insurrection, the defect may be supplied by the following communication, made by a gentleman of accurate information, and of the first respectability in Pennsylvania; who warrants us to assure the public, that *"the plunder of the city of Philadelphia was promised to the Insurgents in 1794, by their leaders."*

The societies of United Irishmen next mark the progress of Illuminism in America. In May, 1798, the declaration and constitution of the American Society of United Irishmen were discovered, and published in Philadelphia. This society was evidently founded on the principles of the illuminated lodges in Europe; and we are not left in the dark as to their object; for no one, who will attentively read their constitution, can hesitate to say, it was to enlist and organize the discontented and factious, and particularly *foreigners,* in the different parts of the United States, in order to diffuse the spirit, and promote the infernal designs, of Illuminism in this country. Their constitution is drawn up with considerable ingenuity. The ostensible object of their association, was to act in concert with their United brethren

---

* Ibid., 12th paragraph.

in Ireland. "*Equality* and *Liberty* to ALL men," was, at the same time, held forth in their declaration; and in their *test*, each member pledged himself, that he would direct all his efforts to the "attainment of *liberty* and *equality to* MANKIND, *in whatever country he may reside.*" The section which immediately follows the *test*, exhibits a strong evidence, that the *ostensible* object of the society, was not the *real* one; and, that under the semblance of humanity, was concealed a project far from the emancipation of mankind. The section is this: "That the *test* of this society, and the *intention* of this *institution*, (in all other respects than as a *social body*, attached to freedom) be considered as *secret* and *inviolable*, in all cases, but between members, and in the body of the society." The existence of this society, the intended secrecy of its designs, and the evident tendency of its labors, exhibit further, and strong proof, that the baneful influence of *Illuminism* is diffusing itself through this country.

Although our ears were daily wounded with the disgusting extravagancies of France, and our property subjected to the most wanton spoilations, still, from some secret cause, her influence was prevailing in America; when the directory, misled by the shameful pliancy of our ambassador,* entirely miscalculated their influence, and the remaining energy of the American character. Sure of their prey, they too soon threw off the mask which concealed their designs. Their conduct toward the American Envoys, who were sent to demand a redress of grievances, was so repugnant to every sentiment of justice, good faith, and propriety, as to admit of no apology. The mist, which had been gathering around the minds of Americans, and through which France appeared great and magnanimous,

---

* Mr. Munroe.

was dissolved in a moment. In vain was recourse had to the deceptive arts which heretofore had been so successful. Her detestable policy silenced her advocates, and united all who regarded righteousness, or felt for the interest, or dignity of their country. A barrier was now formed, which appeared to be a lasting defense against the intriguing spirit of France. We forgot our losses and sufferings in the pleasing prospect that out countrymen would forever escape her deceptive snares. But, alas, these hopes have vanished. Subsequent events, which have lulled the fears, and impaired the energies of our countrymen, have furnished unhappy opportunities to the friends of France, to propagate her principles, and extend her influence, in America; and at no period, perhaps, has their success been greater, than for the last three or four years. What is to be the result, cannot be foreseen.

The influence of WASHINGTON, more extensive, perhaps, than ever one man acquired over a nation, proved, during his administration, a great means, under Providence, of security against the insidious attempts of our enemies, and the progress of self-created societies, of the tendency of which he was aware, and gave faithful warning to his country. At a later period, the full tide of wealth, which has poured in upon almost all classes of citizens has operated as an antidote against the libels of the enemies of our government. But, if these peculiar advantages have scarcely preserved us from the *mortal embraces* of France; if a steady opposition has been made to a government whose measures have been uniformly successful, and murmurs, complaints, and insurrections have marked a period, attended with every soothing circumstance of prosperity, what may we not fear from those pressing difficulties which may arise, and which, probably, will be the result of those luxurious habits we are now forming, when the means of gratification, as they must be, are contracted? What indeed can we expect in any circumstances, should the spirit of Illuminism continue its progress; should our renewed intercourse with France, extend the influence of those principles which have already been too successfully disseminated in America?

Although the observations in this chapter have a political aspect, they have not been introduced with a political design, but in evidence of the progress of the genius of Illuminism, the constant attendant of French influence. France is the region of Illuminism, and her policy and principles are dictated by its spirit. The leading characters in her revolution have publicly avowed the sentiments so industriously propagated by Voltaire, and systematically taught in the school of Weishaupt.

In a discourse, composed by Anacharsis Cloots, and printed and circulated by order of the National Convention, we find the following sentiments. "Man, when free, wants no other divinity than himself. Reason dethrones both the kings of the earth, and the *king of heaven*. No monarchy above, if we wish to preserve *our republic* below. Volumes have been written, to determine whether a republic of Atheists could exist: I maintain, that every other republic is a chimera. If you admit the existence of an heavenly sovereign, you introduce the wooden horse within your walls; what you adore by day, will be your destruction at night."* By virtually abolishing the Christian sabbath, enthroning Reason in the temples of the Deity, and by affixing to their burying-grounds the inscription, *"Death is an everlasting sleep,"* a sentiment expressive of the essence of atheism, the Convention gave the most explicit sanction to the above principles.

This is French liberty; the liberty they wish to propagate. The state of their finances requires that they should be

---

* Residence in France.

more immediately active in promoting revolutions in governments, than in propagating atheism, as every revolution afforded a pretext for plunder, and for demanding contributions; but, in the mean time, they have not been inactive in their attempts to abolish, what they style, "the *tyranny of heaven.*" Their Anti-Christian writings, which have been rapidly circulated, even in these distant regions, and their *Propaganda,* afford ample proofs of their zeal. Girtanner, in his memoirs on the French revolution, estimates "the acting members of the club of the *Propagandists,* at fifty-thousand, and their general fund, in 1791, at thirty-million of livres; that they are extended over the world; having for their object the promotion of revolutions, and the doctrines of atheism. It is a maxim in their code, that it is better to defer their attempts for fifty years, than to fail in them through too much precipitation."*

That the principles of infidelity have attended the progress of French influence in America, does not admit of a doubt. The truth of this remark is evident from inspection. Who can avoid seeing, and who that believes the importance of religion to mankind, can avoid lamenting, the alarming revolution which has taken place here, in the essential doctrines of natural and revealed religion? The sentiment has not yet been openly avowed, but I have satisfying evidence, that it has been more than once asserted, to this effect, that *we never should be free until the Christian church was abolished.*

The two following articles of information were communicated by a gentleman of the first respectability in Pennsylvania, to his correspondent in New England, who has favored me with his letter:† He writes, "On the occa-

---

* Barruel's Memoirs, Vol. II. p. 245.
  † The original is with the author.

sion of the election of citizen McKean, an altar was erected on the commons, on which the statues of liberty and peace were placed. Large libations were poured on the alter by the priests of liberty, who were clothed in white, with red caps, stuck round with sprigs of laurel. After which an ox was sacrificed before the altar, and its flesh divided among a thousand citizens, while many republican toasts were drank by the company. The ox was likewise adorned with garlands, according to the Pagan ritual."

The other article is as follows: "It was lately proposed in Ricket's Circus, (at Philadelphia) to exhibit a view of *Hell,* for the diversion of the good company, and such exhibition would have taken place, had not the combustibles, prepared for the occasion, taken fire too soon, and consumed the house." The first account, the writer says, "is taken from a democratic paper, printed at York (Pennsylvania) and with respect to both," he adds, "You may rely on the accuracy of the information."

The following statement is taken from a printed abstract of the society, for the propagation of the gospel in foreign parts, for the year, ending the 21st February, 1800, and annexed to Dr. Courtenay's anniversary sermon.

"A sect, called New Lights, but composed of the most enthusiastic and extravagant of the different denominations in Nova Scotia, have lately appeared in that province, whose political, are said to be equally dangerous with their religious principles. It is believed that the conductors of these people are engaged in the general plan of a total revolution in religion and civil government; and it is a certain fact, that the Age of Reason, Volney on the Ruin of Empires, and a false representation of the French Revolution, have been secretly handed about by professed New Lights."

Chapter XV.

In Continuation

I N the former chapter, some documents were introduced to prove that the noxious weed of Illuminism had taken root in our happy soil, and was here diffusing a poison, more penetrating and mortal than that of the famous Bohan Upas. Let us now examine the aspect of facts, which are universally known to exist, and observe their agreement with this hypothesis. If all appearances harmonize with the sentiment here advanced, and are unaccountable on every other supposition, this will give much additional weight to the proofs already adduced. Indeed, the evidence resulting from the existing state of things, often impresses the mind with a conviction, no less forcible, than the most positive testimony. This kind of evidence, however, requires an equal balance; its due weight can never be ascertained where the unsteady hand of passion holds the beam, or where prejudice possesses the scale.

Persuaded that there are many of my fellow citizens, who are not guided by prejudice or partiality, I would invite them to a calm and deliberate consideration of the following queries, founded on the state of things among us, as they have existed, and do now exist.

1st. Whence arises the avowed attachment of a numerous party, in this country, to France? Why are we constantly hearing, that she is the only nation in whom we can repose confidence, on whose fidelity we can rely; the only friend of the rights of man? Why are all her enormities so industriously palliated, and her victories celebrated as the triumphs of righteousness?

Perhaps there has never been an instance in the history of man, of a more sincere and disinterested friendship between two nations, than that which once subsisted between American and France; and I hope there is not now a citizen of the United States, who would not feel a sincere and ardent pleasure in the return of that nation to the paths of wisdom, and the enjoyment of the sweets of civil and religious liberty. But what must be in the heart of that man, whose feelings accord with her principles, and who is gratified with the success of her present measures? Must not every friend to society, to order, and religion, adopt, with respect to France, the energetic language of the Patriarch, "O my soul, come not thou into their secret; unto their assembly, mine honor, be not thou united?" Whence then the charm which so strongly binds such a numerous party in this country to France?

Is it their malicious opposition* to the Christian relig-

---

* Sunday, Nov. 17, Anacharsis Cloots did homage to the Convention, and made the following proposal. "It is now become an acknowledged truth, that the adversaries of religion have well deserved of mankind. On this account, I demand, that a statue be erected to the first abjuring priest, in the temple of reason." The proposal of Cloots was referred to a committee, and adopted.

In the same month, on the motion of Chaumette, which was received with applauses, it was resolved in the Council of Paris,

"1. That all the churches and temples of different religions and worship, which are known to be in Paris, shall be instantly shut.

"2. That whatever troubles may ensue in Paris, in consequence of religious motives, the priests and ministers of the different religions, shall each be particularly responsible.

"3. That every person, requiring the opening of a church, or temple, shall be put under arrest, as a suspected person, &c. &c." – Kett on Prophecy, London edition, 1800, Vol. II. p. 240.

ion, burning their bibles,* obliterating the Christian sabbath,† paying divine honors to imaginary deities,‡ and

---

* "What," says an intelligent American gentleman, in a letter to his friend in Boston, dated at Havre, Nov. 24, 1793, "What do our good folks think of dethroning God, *burning the Bible,* and shutting up the churches? Before I came here, they burnt the bible in the public square, pulled down the images of Jesus and Mary, in the churches, and filled the niches with those of *Reason* and *Liberty,* &c." See Dr. Morse's Thanksgiving Sermon, 1798, p. 22.

† "Oct. 25, 1793, a new calendar was proposed, and adopted by the Convention, with a view to obliterate the remembrance, as well as observance of that holy day, which has been, from the earliest times, consecrated to the exercise of public devotion. Festivals were appointed at stated periods, similar to those which were established in times of Idolatry, to the Virtues, to Genius, to Labor, to Opinion, to Rewards." Kett, Vol. II. p. 236. See also, Residence in France, p. 270, New York edition.

‡ "The magnificent church of St. Genevieve, at Paris, was changed, by the National Assembly, into a repository for the remains of their great men, or rather into a pagan temple, and as such, was aptly distinguished by the name of the *Pantheon.*" [N.B. *The Pantheon was a beautiful edifice at Rome, anciently a temple, dedicated to all the Gods.*] "To this temple, the remains of Voltaire and of Rosseau were conveyed in solemn and magnificent procession. The bones of Voltaire were placed upon the high altar, and incense was offered. And when the infatuated multitude bowed down before the relics of this arch-enemy of Christ, in silent adoration, a voice, a single voice, was heard to utter, in a tone of agony and indignation, these memorable words; *O God, thou wilt be revenged!* Search was immediately made for the man, who thus dared to interrupt these rites, and this Abdiel was, probably, sacrificed to the fury of the multitude." Kett, Vol. II. p. 233.

"Previous to the tenth day, on which a celebration was to take place, a deputy arrived, accompanied by the female goddess; that is, (if the town itself did not produce one for the purpose) a Roman dress, of white satin, was hired from the theater, with which she was invested, her head was covered with a red cap, ornamented with oak leaves, one arm was reclined on a plough, the other grasped a spear, and her feet were supported by a globe and environed by mutilated emblems of feodality.

"Thus equipped, the divinity and her appendages were borne on the shoulders of Jacobins '*en bonnet rouge,*' and escorted by the national countenancing, even in their National Assembly, the most impious blasphemies against the God of Heaven?*

Has France recommended herself to our esteem by those horrid murders, and scenes of carnage and blood, which spared neither the hoary head, the innocent suppli-cating female, nor the harmless infant, but added wanton barbarity to her pretended acts of justice;† and persecuted

---

guard, mayor, judges, and all the constituted authorities, who, whether diverted or indignant, were obliged to preserve a respectful gravity of exterior. When the whole cavalcade arrived at the place appointed, the goddess was placed on an altar erected for the occasion, from whence she harangued the people, who, in return, proffered their adoration, and sung the *Carmagnole,* and other republican hymns of the same kind. They then proceeded in the same order to the principal church, in the choir of which the same ceremonies were renewed; a priest was procured to abjure his faith, and avow the whole of Christianity an imposture, and the festival concluded with the burning of prayer books, saints, confessionals, and everything appropriated to the use of public worship. The greater part of the attendants looked on in silent terror and astonishment; while others, intoxicated, or probably paid to act the scandalous farce, danced around the flames, with an appearance of frantic and savage mirth. It is not to be forgotten, that representatives of the people, often presided as the high priests of these rites; and their official dispatches to the Convention, in which these ceremonies were minutely described, were always heard with bursts of applause, and sanctioned by degrees of insertion in the *Bulletin,* a kind of official newspaper, distributed at the expense of government, in large towns, and posted up in public places." See Residence in France, p. 270, New York edition.

* "Nov. 1793, the pupils of the new republican school, of the section des Areis, appeared at the bar, and one of them set forth, that all religious worship had been suppressed in his section, even to the very idea of religion. He added that *he and his school fellows detested God,* and that, instead of learning scripture, they learned the declaration of rights. The president having expressed to the deputation the satisfac-tion of the Convention, they were admitted to the honors of the sitting, amidst the loudest applause." Kett, p. 224.

† "Sept. 2, 1792. The people broke open the prison of the Abbaye, and commenced a massacre of the prisoners. Many had been confined

the ministers of religion with marks of peculiar rancor?*

---

on slight suspicions; many poor priests, on no particular accusation, but merely because they were priests.   The same horrid scenes were extended to all the prisons in Paris.

"Among the unhappy victims who suffered on this occasion, was Madame de Lamballe, whose only crime was, the friendship of the queen. She was struck on the head with the bludgeon of one assassin, and her head separated from her body with the saber of another. The body, after a series of indignities, not to be related, was trailed by the mob through the streets." Moore's Journal, Boston edition, Vol. I. p. 183-189.

Kett, describing the same event, says, "Three successive nights and days, scarcely measured their assassinations of prepared victims, who had been, from motives of private hatred and revenge, imprisoned. Seven thousand six hundred and five persons were inhumanly murdered, *and the assassins publicly demanded their wages.* During the short interval between these bloody scenes, the passions of the populace were fired; the relentless Roland had the care of the general police; the bloody Danton was the minister of justice; the insidious Petion was mayor of Paris, and the treacherous Manuel was procurator of the common hall. These magistrates were evidently, either the authors, or the accessories, of these massacres." Kett, Vol. II. p. 235.

"A fourth of these, our representatives," says the author of La Conjuration, page 160, "ripped open the wombs of the mothers; tore out the palpitating embryo, to deck the point of a pike of liberty and equality." Many instances of the like nature might be produced, but I am not willing to torture the feelings of the reader.

* The commissioner Garnier wrote thus to the Convention, on the 11th of December, 1793: "I have caused fifty-eight priests to be drowned." The next month he writes again, "Ninety priests have just been brought to me; I have drowned them, *which has given me great pleasure.*" "It appears that there have been two millions of persons murdered in France, since it has called itself a republic; among whom are reckoned 250,000 women, 230,000 children (besides those murdered in the womb) and 24,000 Christian priests, many of them Protestants." Kett, Vol. II. p. 252.

The conflagration of 1820 towns, villages, and hamlets, in one portion of its own territory; the deliberate assassination of women and children, by hundreds and by thousands; the horrid pollution of female victims, expiring or expired; and the establishment of a tan yard, under

Or are they pleased with the loose morality of France;* where the sacred obligations of the marriage covenant are dissolved;† prostitution countenanced;‡ suicide publicly applauded;§ where dissipation meets with no check, and the endearing charities of life are extinguished?** Do these

---

the auspices of government, for manufacturing leather out of the skins of the murdered citizens, are facts, which exclusively grace the blood stained annals of the Gallic republic, and give to the revolution a dreadful pre-eminence in guilt." Kett, Vol. II. p. 251.

* "To keep the minds of the Parisians in the fever of dissolute gaiety, they are at more expense, from the national treasury, for the support of the sixty theaters, than all the pensions and honorary offices in Britain, three times told, amount to. Between the 10th of August, 1792, and the 1st of January, 1794, upwards of 200 *new* plays were acted in the Parisian theaters. Their *immorality* and their barbarism exceed all description." Kett, Vol. II. p. 253.

† "In consequence of the decree relative to marriage, it is calculated, that, in 1793, one hundred and fifty divorces took place in every month in Paris." Kett, Vol. II. p. 253.

‡ "By a decree of the Convention, June 6, 1794, it is declared that there is nothing criminal in the promiscuous commerce of the sexes." Kett, Vol. II. p. 217.

§ "Beaurepaire shot himself at the surrender of Verdun. When the news reached the National Assembly, M. Delaunay proposed, that his remains should be brought from St. Menehold, and interred in a French Pantheon. This was immediately decreed, and an honorary inscription put on his tomb." Moore, Vol. I. p. 238.

** "A man, or rather a monster, named Phillippe, came to the Jacobin club, of which he was a member; and, with a box in his hand, mounted the tribune. Here he made a long speech on patriotism, concluding by a declaration, that he looked upon everyone who preferred the ties of blood and of nature, to patriotic duty, as an aristocrat worthy of death; and to convince them of the purity and sincerity of his own principles, he opened the box, and held up by the grey hair, the bloody and shriveled heads of his father and mother, which, said the impious wretch, I have cut off because they obstinately persisted in not hearing mass from a constitutional priest. The speech of this patricide received the loudest applauses." Le Historic du Clergé François, or, History of the French Clergy, p. 328.

persons find the traits of a *great* nation in the cruel exactions practiced in Holland; in the perfidious dealing with
the Swiss; or the detestable arts by which Geneva was
subjugated to her will?   Has she recommended herself to

The following information was communicated in a letter from a
gentlemen of the first respectability in Europe, to his friend in the
United States, dated Sept. 1800.

"I cannot refrain from mentioning another particular. A count
Soden, proprietor of lands on the borders of the Black Forest, has
several small Iron Works on his estates, which occasioned him to be
continually riding from place to place during the stay of Jourdan's army,
in that country, in 1796. He published, at Nuremburg, an account of his
own observations.   He had many transactions with the different
detachments who ravaged that country, so that he was perfectly
acquainted with the state and conduct of that army. He says, that to
keep the army always in good humor, there was a fund for a theater, and
concerts of music, and balls, at every headquarters, and that a liberal
allowance was granted to the officers who took with them their wives
and mistresses. Each had as many bed-fellows as he could support by
his plunder. The ladies, of course, were the patronesses of every gaiety
and elegance.   But lying in, and particularly, nursing, was altogether
incompatible with this plan of the National Councils. The only remedy
for this, which occurred to their wisdom, was *(horresco referens!) to
drown the newborn infants,* — to DROWN THEM!!! This was actually
done under military escort. A sergeant and party of soldiers accompanied the murders, and protected them from the peasants. Count Soden
did not see any of these sacrifices with his own eyes, but he saw two of
the innocent victims, and he heard several of these accounts in a way
that he could not doubt of their truth. In particular, he saw a clergyman, at a village about 12 English miles from Nuremburg, who being
also a magistrate, attempted to hinder the perpetration of the horrid
deed. The soldiers threw him into the river, and fired some shots at him
and at those who saved him. He was so fortunate as to save the little
innocent, and took it to his house and provided a nurse for it. The
mother went away next day, with the rest of the party, but stayed seven
weeks at a little town five miles off, and in all that time, never once sent
to inquire whether this issue of her own blood was dead or alive. All
this is published by Count Soden, and his name affixed as a voucher for
the truth of it. I defy the annals of human debasement to match this."

Americans by her determination to plunder us of our property?* By her meditated attack on the southern states,† or by those unprovoked depredations on our commerce, condemned by a most respectable member of their legislature, as equally inconsistent with good faith, and sound policy?‡

Not admitting the above as the foundation of their attachment to France, her partisans will probably rather recur to their usual plea, which, however destitute of substance, has a more reputable aspect, viz. gratitude, yes *gratitude,* never to be cancelled, for her afforded protection. It is no small trial of patience to be compelled to answer pleas, which have no foundation in reason, nor even in the mind of the person who makes them; and which are brought forward merely to conceal less honorable sentiments. It is very easy to answer in the present case, that if gratitude is still due for assistance, for which the stipulated price has been paid in full, and which was afforded, as everyone must be sensible, and as the National Assembly have acknowledged, not from a regard to the interests of republicanism, but from opposition to England, this gratitude is due to the ancient, and not to the present government of France; and ought to lead us to deplore the fate of an unhappy king, and not to attach us to those who, with circumstances of needless and unfeeling cruelty, have deprived him of his crown and life.§

---

* See Barlow's Letter, March 1, 1798.
† Harper's Address of March 3, 1799.
‡ Pastoret's motion in the Council of 500, 1797.
§ Among many instances in confirmation of this fact, it is sufficient to observe, "that the head of the princess Lamballe was hoisted on a pike, and carried before the temple where the royal family were imprisoned, and they were called to the window to see it. A fainting fit, from hearing of the event, fortunately saved the queen from the heart-rending sight." See Moore's and Clery's Journals.

Or will they justify their partiality for France by the plea, that it is a *sister republic;* the land of liberty? It is styled, indeed, a republic, but in reality, a more despotic government does not exist in Europe. From the beginning of the revolution the people have been the dupes of successive factious leaders, who have misled one part by false representations, and drove the other by terror into a compliance with their ambitious views. But now, their government is in theory, as well as practice, despotic. However favorable to the natural rights of men, we may believe the several constitutions successively adopted in the years 1791, 1793, and 1795, to have been, the present leaves the people but a very faint semblance of representation or legislative power. Are we not then warranted in presuming that, among the more enlightened citizens, at least, the real grounds of attachment to France, are different from the ostensible ones?

2nd. To what other cause, than the one here suggested, can we ascribe that opposition to all the leading measures of the late administration, which has been uniformly maintained by those identical persons, who have manifested such a strange predilection for French politics? The notoriety of this opposition, renders it unnecessary to adduce any proofs of its existence. That our rulers have committed errors, is presumable. They were human beings, and had to explore a new, and untried path, amidst innumerable difficulties, without the useful aid of precedent and experience. But were those errors such as afforded any just pretext for the perpetual clamors, the factions, cabals, and insurrections, with which they have been opposed, and impeded? Whatever may have been their errors, the result of their measures has been the establishment of peace with the nations of Europe; peace with the Indians upon the principles of humanity, and with the prospects of permanency; the preservation of our neutrality against artful and violent attempts to involve us in European contentions; the consolidation of our feeble union, and the restoration of that vigor and energy which were almost exhausted. Our deranged finances have been reduced to a regular system, and a revenue raised, which, though scarcely perceived in its operation, has been adequate to the support of government, has answered many extraordinary demands, and effected a considerable reduction of the public debt. To the same judicious system, are we indebted for the existence of a *Navy,* which has enabled us to repel many wanton encroachments on our neutral rights, and been the principal means of our present commercial prosperity. Favorable arrangements were also made for the recovery of our property from the hands of spoilers; and that this provision has not been more complete has probably been owing to the belief which the French government entertained of their influence in the United States. With great justness, President JEFFERSON announced, in his inaugural speech, that our government, at the close of our late administration, was "in the full tide of *successful* experiment."

I shall not attempt a further justification of those measures which have been so severely censured. All who have witnessed the difficulties from which we have been extricated; and the prosperity which has resulted to all classes of citizens, from the measures which have been adopted and pursued, in the two late administrations, and yet remain unsatisfied, as to their wisdom, I can have no hope of convincing by any arguments I can use. It ought, however, to be remarked, that these measures were adopted by WASHINGTON and ADAMS, and warmly recommended by them, as indispensable to the peace and prosperity of the Unites States, and the perpetuity of their union and independence. We may probably soon be called to witness the effects of a departure from their salutary system.

To what cause then are we to attribute the opposition

which has been made to such men, and such measures; men, who have given the most unequivocal proofs of a wise, patriotic, and faithful adherence to the principles of rational liberty, and the interests of America, through scenes which try men's principles; measures, which have procured this country, respectability abroad, and prosperity and strength at home? The nature and systematic operations of this opposition appear perfectly unaccountable and mysterious, unless we recur to some *secret* influence. This influence, moving many hidden springs, produces these uniform effects which are visible in all parts of our country. And this conclusion forces itself upon our minds when we recollect, that the class of men who raise this outcry, and who are so extremely jealous of any encroachments on the privileges of mankind, are the very persons who justify all the extravagant and tyrannical proceedings of the French government; not excepting that arbitrary act of the directory, in 1797, which drove into banishment, without the form of a trial, some of the best of her legislators, and the most worthy of her citizens.

3rd. Whence is it, that this jealous concern for the liberties of America, the nice sense of the rights of man, (to which is ascribed the opposition to government) originated in the southern States, is still most prevalent there, and is thence communicated to the eastern States? I certainly have no disposition to foment a spirit of division, nor would I suggest an idea detracting from the respect due to many southern gentlemen, whose fortunes have been devoted to the pursuits, not of pleasure, but of the liberal arts, and who have become blessings and ornaments to their country; but, as an opposition in principles is known to exist, it becomes necessary, in order to acquire just notions of liberty, that the origin and tendency of these principles should be freely discussed. Some observations on the subject are evidently of importance in the present inquiry. I must, therefore, take the liberty of asking, if the principles, which have attached many citizens of the United States to France, and rendered them opposed to the leading measures adopted by WASHINGTON and ADAMS, flow from an enlightened spirit of freedom, whence is it, that these sentiments are found, originally, and principally, in the southern part of the Union?

Are the habits and manners of the people there, more congenial to the spirit of genuine republicanism? Or are the citizens generally better informed? Do they acquire this patriotic spirit in their elective assemblies, where, we have been informed, by one of their own legislators, that bludgeons are substituted for proxies, and the arguments of the citizens acquire weight in proportion to their bodily strength and activity? In drawing the portrait of a true republican, would you represent him with one hand contending for the rights of man, and with the other holding a scourge over his trembling slave?

It has been supposed of the first importance in republican governments, that the lower classes of the people be well informed; that youth be taught to subject their passions to the dictates of reason and duty, and be early trained to the habits of virtue, industry, and economy. But if, as has been represented, New England be the "*La Vendee* of America," and its inhabitants aristocrats, until they are politically regenerated by the southern states, the above principles of education must be renounced as erroneous, and the race ground, and the gaming table, acknowledged the best school for the education of republicans.

Here new paradoxes occur, and paradoxes they remain till we recollect, that Illuminism first dawned upon the southern states; that they formed the principal resort for European emigrants, and there only, we discover the lodges which derive their origin from the *Grand Orient,* at Paris. Have we, then, no grounds to conclude that these outrageous pretenders to liberty, who "dispise government, and are not afraid to speak evil of dignities," are the genuine offspring of that sect, which we have seen alike opposed to the restraints of religion, and the laws of the society?

Why do we hear, from the same quarter, the clergy of New England represented, not only as useless, but a public nuisance.* I shall not undertake the defense of this order of men, nor attempt a refutation of the various, and very indefinite charges brought against them. The people of New England are acquainted with the clergy, and can judge for themselves, whether or not they are justly censured. One charge, however, as it is more frequently alleged, and respects their secret intentions, and therefore not so easily refuted, demands more particular attention. The charge to which I refer, is, in substance, this, that they are unfriendly to the political interests of their country, and the principles of the American revolution. Is this a fact? If it be proved, I presume it must be by the same kind of logic, by which those who bring the charge, attempt to prove that WASHINGTON was blind to the interests of his country; ADAMS, a monarchist; and the citizens of New England, aristocrats. But let us attend to facts.

It is a matter of public notoriety, that at the time of the American revolution, no class of men were more united, or more active in their efforts to promote that cause. Their public performances afforded, also, abundant proofs of their warm attachment to the French revolution, until it became evident that the cause in which France had embarked, was the cause of licentiousness, oppression, and atheism. Have then these men in a body relinquished that

---

* In proof of the fact here intimated, I beg leave to refer the reader to those newspapers in which Washington's system of politics is condemned, and the measures of France advocated in the gross.

system of political faith, which, at that period, they so fervently embraced? To what probable cause, can such a general revolution of sentiment be attributed?

Their accusers will not probably ascribe it to their ignorance, for they likewise accuse them of meddling too much with politics; it is therefore presumable that they have, at least, acquired political information.

Will it be said that the prospects of ambition have led them astray? This would be a very uncharitable supposition indeed; for although they are *men of like passion* with others, they are not, in all cases, exposed to *like* temptations. Excluded, by their profession, from posts of worldly honor and profit, they are merely spectators of the contentions of ambition. Unless they are influenced by a patriotic concern for their countrymen, they have no connection with government, other than to secure for themselves the blessings of freedom, and to transmit the precious inheritance to their posterity. In haste to deprive them of public confidence, their accusers have industriously, and indiscriminately applied to the clergy here, the charges brought against the order in Europe. But what similarity in situation is there between the cardinals, bishops, and lords spiritual, of the European hierarchies, and an American clergyman, who, by the scantiness of his support is compelled to the most rigid economy, and often to labor with his own hands, to obtain a decent support for his dependants; and instead of the prospect of preferment, must consider himself fortunate if he be not dispossessed of his office, and subjected to the inconveniences of a removal?

Their poverty, indeed, exposes them to temptations, in point of property, should such temptations present; but it is fortunate, with respect to this charge, that the public measures to which they have conscientiously given their support, have been unfavorable to their private interests. The duties of imposts and excise, which are taken from the consumer, and the establishment of banks, which has operated greatly to advance the price of every article of life, have reduced their means of subsistence. This has been so obvious, that their parishioners, in general, have felt themselves bound in justice to increase the nominal sum, to preserve the original value of their stipends. The clergy, alone, are excluded a share in the increasing wealth of their country; and were they governed by selfish motives, merely, would be the first to oppose, rather than the first to defend the administration.

But it has also been suggested, that, in espousing this cause, they have meanly courted the favor of the majority. For an answer to this charge, facts declare the truth; for it is a known fact, that many of the clergy have nobly maintained their sentiments, and warned their hearers of their danger, at the hazard of their displeasure, and of offending particular gentlemen of influence. The author in particular, pleases himself, that he, at least, shall escape the charge of a time-server, as he is weekly notified, through the medium of the Worcester Gazette, by one high in office, that the cause he here advocates, is fast sinking into contempt; and that he already foresees the "downfall of Federal Clergymen."

The above observations are not so much designed to vindicate the clerical order, as to develop the real designs of their calumniators. These accusations appear as groundless as the attachment of their authors to French politics. It is to be presumed that they are not the real causes of the present opposition to the clergy of New England. No; their attachment to order, the resistance they make to the progress of philsophism, their exertions in defense of Christianity, and their attempts to impress its important, but unwelcome truths, on mankind, constitute their real crime, in the judgment of their accusers. Political opinions prove a convenient cover for schemes not yet ripe for execution. Were the enemies of religion among us to come forward unmasked, and avow their real designs, it would be demonstrative proof that they had apostatized from the principles of their master; but the disciples of Voltaire and Weishaupt are true to their favorite maxims, "to bind men with *invisible* bands. To strike, but hide the hand."

We accordingly find those who are endeavoring to deprive the clergy of all public confidence, abounding in what D'Alembert calls *"bows to religion."* Religion is carefully spoken of with high respect, in those publications which denounce the body of the clergy as hostile to the interests of their country. "They must be gained or ruined," the reader will recollect, is a prime maxim of the order; but finding that the clergy of New England will not be induced to betray their religion and country, and consign themselves and their posterity to infamy and wretchedness, they are unceasingly represented, as attempting to subvert those establishments to which they have invariably given their support, and to annex to their office the honors and emoluments which are peculiar to the corrupt religious establishments in Europe.

That friends to order and religion, by a series of misrepresentations, are led to give their support to systems, which, if free from deception, they would detest, is not to be doubted; but the man who approves the principles on which the French revolution has been conducted, and is pleased with that liberty and independence, which have received the sanction of the National Assembly, cannot but wish for the abolition of the Christian faith, and whatever gives it support.

The reader will remark, that the same evidence which proves that Illuminism, or French influence, (for one involves the other) has existed in America, proves that it now exists among us. The similarity of the effect, indicates the sameness of the cause. In 1794, we find Fauchet sketching the grievances which excited the western insurrection. In 1797, appeared the societies of United Irishmen. In the same year, the American Envoys were assured, "That it was in vain for them to think of uniting their countrymen against France, by exposing the unreasonableness of their demands. You ought to know," they are told, "that the *diplomatic skill* of France, and the *means she possesses in your country,* are sufficient to enable her, with *the French party in America,* to throw the blame which will attend the rupture of the negotiations, on the federalists; and you may assure yourselves this will be done."*

At the same period, Mr. Pinckney was told by another French negotiator, "we know we have a considerable party in America, who are strongly in our interests."† Has this "French party in America," this "very considerable party," on which the Directory placed so much dependence in 1797, became entirely extinct? Have they been in no degree active, since that period, to excite jealousies, foment divisions, alienate the citizens from their best friends, to disseminate the principles of infidel philosophy, and overturn the ancient happy establishments of our country?

If, in their attempts to deprive us of our religion, they have not obtained an equally decided victory, zeal has not been wanting, nor has their success been inconsiderable. The principal bulwarks are yet safe. Our bibles are not consigned to the flames; nor our places of worship devoted to idolatry, and pagan rites. The Christian sabbath, although treated with practical contempt by some who ought to give it their firm and decided support, is not yet abolished by law. But many of the outworks are in the power of the enemy, and they are daily making regular and alarming

---

* Dispatches from American Envoys, published by the Secretary of State, No. 2.

† Ibid., Exhibit A. No. 4.

approaches.

It is not my intention, by the foregoing observations, to implicate all those who err in their political opinions, as engaged in the conspiracy against Christianity, and social order. This is far from being the case; yet I have no doubt that many persons, who are sincere friends to religion, their country, and mankind, are led, by a series of misrepresentations, to give their support to systems, which, if seen in their true nature and tendency, would excite their abhorrence. It is, indeed, astonishing that good characters, real friends to Christianity, should be so easily filled with suspicion and jealously towards men of established character, for piety, talents, and patriotism, and drawn in to aid the enemies of their religion and their country; and this too, by persons, whose moral and religious characters they cannot but hold in abhorrence; but Weishaupt himself wondered at the success of his own policy, and in his confidential epistles, often exclaims, "What cannot men be made to believe."

Persuaded that many are unwarily led to advocate a cause which militates against the best interests of their country, these historical sketches, and articles of evidence, have been collected for their benefit; and with the same friendly design their calm and unprejudiced attention is requested to the contents of the following.

Address

Friends, and Fellow Citizens,

I am very sensible that the discerning eye will discover many defects in the foregoing statement, but they are errors of the head, not of the heart. There is not a circumstance intentionally misrepresented, nor a sentiment expressed, which is not the result of conviction. I am aware that some from policy, and others from sentiment, will be disposed to treat these apprehensions as chimerical; but to me they are real. In my view, alarming dangers hang over my country, and even now the lurking foe is preparing an explosion, which, unless prevented, will level her rising glories with the dust. Possessing these sentiments, neither duty nor patriotism would suffer me to decline a service, however ungrateful, which afforded some prospect of aiding a cause to which I feel myself connected by the strongest ties of affection. Your country, is my country; here I have a family, dear to me, and friends, whose fortune, with my own, is connected with that of America. Can I then see her dangers, and be silent?

Warmly has my heart entered into the pleasing prospects which have dawned upon the land of my nativity, nor will I yet despair of her salvation, confiding in that helping hand, which has been her guide in darkness, and her shield in danger. Numerous and powerful still are her friends, could they be roused to exertion; and exertion there must be, or our ruin is inevitable. If propitious heaven has decreed salvation for our country, means will be found to dispel the fascinating charm which is now drawn her into the ravenous jaws of her devourer. She will be enabled to distinguish *real* from *pretended* friends. While we are supine and indolent, resting in the goodness of our cause, and fondly hearkening to those who cry peace and safety, the enemies of our peace, of our independence, of our religion, are alert and restless. It is painful and alarming to hear worthy citizens applauding themselves for the sagacious discovery, that the commotions of the day are merely agitations excited by contending candidates; that we are all aiming, in different ways, at the same object; "that we are all federalists, all republicans." These sentiments, industriously propagated by those who wish to lull us into security, unfortunately accord with that love of ease, so unhappily prevalent in our most important concerns.

Under a like paralytic stupor, the effect of French intrigue, and modern illumination, the Helvetic republic fell a prey to her treacherous invaders. "The inhabitants seemed fearful of being roused from their indifference, and were offended at predictions meant to put them on their guard. Woe to him who disturbed the general quiet by peevish reasoning on the future, and on the danger of connections in which they were sinking deeper and deeper! The majority of the Swiss were like those patients who are angry with the physician for describing their disorder to them."* "We come among you as friends. We are your brothers. Do not be afraid of any ill treatment. Property and persons shall be protected, as much as the enemies of

---

* Mallet du Pan's Destruction of the Helvetic Republic, Boston edition, 1799. p. 108. A book that ought now to be read by every American.

liberty shall be made to suffer."* This was the language of Mengaud, commissioner of the Executive Directory, in his proclamation, prefaced with "Peace and safety to all his friends." The too credulous Swiss greedily drank the luscious poison; they believed that the Directory were, what they pretended to be, friends to freedom, and the rights of man. They even banished their faithful monitor, when he endeavored to awaken them to a sense of their danger. But *"imprisonments, insults, rapes, requisitions, and rapine* of all kinds, signalized the arrival of these strangers, whom *Mengaud* had but just announced to their victims *as brothers and friends."*†

Confide not, my countrymen, in an imaginary power to resist the subtle invaders, when once they have bound your hands with invisible bands. Your enemies themselves have forewarned you, "that an army of *principles* will prevail, where an army of *soldiers* cannot."‡ When they have sufficiently corrupted your morals, philosophized your religion, overturned your ancient establishments, and disseminated their disorganizing principles among you, then will they rise upon their prey, and add American to the list of *"fleeced"* republics.

Mallet Du Pan, describing the situation of Switzerland, previous to the late revolution there, observes, "There was no State in Europe so secure from the contagion of French principles; everything was an antidote to this pestilence: The slow and phlegmatic character of the inhabitants, their rooted and powerful habits, the experience of a government adapted to their dispositions; and, in fine, the soundness of their judgments, which guarded them against the seduc-

---

* Ibid., p. 256.
† Mallet du Pan's Destruction of the Helvetic Republic, p. 147.
‡ Thomas Paine.

tions of the pen, and of the tongue." If such examples will not teach, nor such warnings alarm us, our ruin is not far distant.

It is a false and dangerous sentiment that "monarchies alone have cause to dread the revolutionizing spirit of the times;" for it is obvious that republics are the theaters on which political mountebanks most successfully exhibit their disorganizing feats. Where, as in such governments, popular elections are frequent, and the poison which infects a distant member, is instantly conveyed to the vitals. When an individual is gained, a lodgment is made in the government, of which that individual forms a part, either in person, or by his agent; and his influence is instantaneously felt. In monarchical governments it is very different. The disease, which there pervades the external parts, but very remotely affects the vital, active powers of government. How feeble the impression which France was able to make upon England, compared with the shock which the republics of Europe received from her revolutionary agents? The combination of *United Irishmen,* and similar societies in England and Scotland, produced no visible alteration in the British government; but had it been similar to the American, a complete revolution must have been the consequence.

The same cause which renders republics more accessible to these evils, proportionally prevents their suppression; for those dangerous persons form directly or indirectly, that very power on which society depends to expel the foe; and hence, the government, in this respect, is reduced to a nullity. Nor is a large number of conspirators necessary to raise obstructions and impede the government; for in every society these persons find many natural allies, ever ready to join their forces. Such are disappointed candidates, who are commonly willing rather to impede and perplex, than to assist their more successful competitors; such are those, and they are not a small party, who, from a natural jealousy of their rulers, are prepared to credit every unfavorable intimation concerning them, however improbable or absurd. Such, in fine, are those selfish beings, whom no considerations of public good will induce to act with any vigor: These, if they do not appear in direct opposition to government, are so many clogs and impediments to its vigilance and activity. These plain observations are introduced to awaken you, my countrymen, to that virtuous watchfulness and firmness, necessary to preserve a free government, and to put you upon your guard against the disorganizing arts of those, who, under whatever pretext, are endeavoring to overturn the systems and establishments which experience has taught you are useful.

Do you ask, what is to be done? As uncommon abilities and penetration are less useful in a search after happiness, than upright intentions and an honest heart, I shall attempt an answer to the suggested inquiry. The ingredients of mental and social happiness, like the necessities of life, consist in simples, and are easily obtained. When the theorizing geniuses of the day have invented a better medium of respiration than the vital air, or a bodily ailment preferable to that which nature provides, then will they merit a hearing, while they promise us a *Utopia* in the regions of infidelity, and quiet repose on the billows of revolutions. But if you wish for that kind of order and quietness, for which our favored land has been distinguished, the following directions point out a plain and safe path.

1st. Attend to the education of your children, and let it be your principal care to impress their minds with religious and moral truth. Much has been said, and much more might be pertinently said, upon the importance of education. The youthful mind is a field prepared for the reception of precious seed; but if neglected, will soon be overspread with every poisonous growth. I am convinced that faithful endeavors to instill the principles of virtue and religion into the minds of youth, is attended with a much greater probability of success than is usually imagined. It is undeniable, that early impressions, which have appeared to be entirely erased by the influence of strong passions and peculiar temptations, have survived the shock, and produced the happiest effects. Even where this is not attained, early habits of regularity, decency, and industry, are not of small importance in society, nor are they easily lost. The impressions made by such an education have evidently had a great effect in preventing the influence of the disorganizing principles of the day, in New England states.

A religious education was formerly reprobated by infidels, under the pretence that it gave a bias to the mind before the judgment was matured; but they themselves have removed this objection; they are not ashamed to make it a maxim in their code, to seize the young, untutored mind, and infuse into the unsuspecting heart the poison of atheism. Learn from your enemies the importance of early impressions, and while they are attempting to disseminate the seeds of infidelity, let it be your watchful care to introduce the vigorous plants of piety and virtue. Furnish their minds with useful knowledge; teach them the true dignity of man; read to them the lessons of experience, habituate them to self government, the regulation of their passions, and a ready submission to needful restraints. Attend to their books, and exclude the numerous publications which are either secretly, or avowedly, designed to propagate the immoral and irreligious spirit of the times; or, if this is not practicable, let them not be without the antidote furnished in many late able replied to the pleas of infidelity. We deny our profession as Christians, if it is not our first concern, in the education of our children, to impress their minds with the fear of God; to establish them in the principles of natural and revealed religion, and the evidences of the Christian faith.

The task of forming the youthful mind, at all times one of the most important duties in society, acquires, in present circumstances, an increased demand on our attention. Religion, society, parental affection, unite in the demand. It would be happy, if present dangers should prove the means of awakening the attention of the Christian world, to a subject so deplorably neglected.

It is fervently to be hoped, in particular, that our Colleges, and other literary institutions, will be preserved from contamination. These are principal objects in the view of the modern enemies of mankind. In observing the weakness of human nature, they have discovered, that a youth of genius, thirsting for literary fame, whose education was unfinished, and his judgment immatured, was precisely in a situation to be impressed with the fascinating charms of Illuminism, and prepared to exchange his understanding and conscience, for the flattering title of a philosopher. Much depends, at this day, upon the guardians of our public seminaries, and much we expect from their fidelity and zeal, in preserving these public fountains from impurities.

2nd.   Support those institutions of your ancestors, which you have seen crowned with peace, glory, and happiness. When will mankind receive instruction so forcibly impressed by universal history, by daily observation, and the word of God, that *"Righteousness alone exalteth a nation?"* That rank atheism is destructive to society, receives a ready assent from those who appear insensible of what is equally true, that a departure from the habits and principles of strict virtue and religion, is an approximation to atheism, and a departure from the only solid foundation of social order and peace. They forget that it is religion, not in theory, but in practice, which constitutes the happiness of an individual, and of a nation.

Men who derive their importance from showy accomplishments, and the gewgaws of life, look with contempt upon the simple manners of our venerable ancestors; but whatever advancements we have made in useful discoveries and the elegant arts of life, justice requires that we ascribe to their virtues our most precious blessings. In a strict attention to family government, in early habits of industry, in a sincerity, simplicity, and temperance of manners, and in the civil, literary, and religious establishments of our country, they laid the foundations of what remains of glory and strength in the American edifice. We do not ascribe to them perfection. Human nature will be attended with the characteristics of weakness. In them, a zeal for the truth degenerated into a degree of intolerance; but have not we rushed with violence into the opposite and more dangerous extreme? The narrow path of virtue is stretched to an almost unbounded width; and in these days of Catholicism, the idea that infidelity disqualifies for public offices, or even for future happiness, is condemned as a species of bigotry. It is easy to perceive that such a relaxation of moral and religious principles is, in its effects, a near approach to atheism. The checks necessary to restrain the strong corruptions of the heart are taken away, and these corruptions, as they gain strength, gradually undermine, and, in their progress, will demolish the strongest bulwarks of society.

When an individual loses his habits of industry, acquires a relish for expensive living, and seeks in scenes of dissipation that satisfaction which he no longer finds in the sober pleasures of life, we foresee his ruin, and withdraw our confidence; and can a society composed of such individuals, be long prosperous and happy? No; the ruin is more inevitable in the latter case, than in the former; for a profligate individual may be controlled, perhaps reformed, by his sober neighbors, but when vicious manners become prevalent in society, a current is opened which defies all restraint, and carries along with it, many who nobly attempted to resist its impulse.

I am painfully conscious that the puritanic simplicity of our ancestors, will rather excite a sneer of contempt, than a desire of imitation in this self-important age. Enjoying the full tide of prosperity, moderation, temperance, and the restraints of religion, are unwelcome themes: But this, my countrymen, is the alternative established in the high unalterable decrees of Heaven, if we participate in the *vices* which have wrought the ruin of other nations, we must also partake of *their plagues!*

It will doubtless be understood that these observations are not designed to recommend any particular uncouthness of manners, which the customs of the age, or their peculiar circumstances produced. The value of a gem is not diminished by a polished surface. What principally demands our attention and imitation in our worthy progenitors is, their love of religion, and their strict practical regard to its duties, producing undisguised sincerity, and genuine patriotism. Religion gave direction, vigor, and activity to all their measures. Religion first generated, and that alone can preserve, the glory of America.

Guard this treatise with peculiar care. Here let it be remembered, the efforts of your enemies are secretly, but powerfully directed; and never will they feel their victory complete until, as they themselves express their hope, *"Christianity is thrown into the background."* To this object they are equally prompted by their enmity to the holy nature of this religion, and by a desire to extend their influence over the mind; for they cannot be insensible, that while virtue exists in the world, their system must meet opposition.

But what are the considerations by which these men would induce us to renounce a religion, of the authenticity and benign influence of which, we have such convincing proofs? Modern infidels appear to have placed their principal dependence on the articles, *priestcraft* and *prejudice.*

Under the *first,* they paint, in glowing colors, the pride, ambition, and oppressions of the papal hierarchy, and of the higher orders in other religious establishments. That the emoluments, injudiciously annexed to the clerical office in many parts of Europe, should induce men, destitute of religion, to assume the sacerdotal character, is perfectly agreeable to the known principles of human nature; and that such men, when in office, should disregard their solemn engagements, is very probable; but the conclusion these modern reasoners deduce from these premises, viz., that the Christian religion is a system of priestcraft, is not so clear. If, by ascribing religion to priestcraft they mean, that these wicked priests invented the religion taught in the gospel, the absurdity of the idea, must be apparent to every person acquainted with its holy, humble doctrines. It could not be *craft,* but the highest degree of stupidity, in such men to invent a religion, which, in the strongest terms, condemns their ambitions, and holds them up to mankind as imposters.

If they mean, that the misconduct of some of its ministers and professors proves that Christianity is a fable, the inference is equally erroneous; for is it evident, that if revelation be true, hypocrisy would have had no existence, or that ambitious men would not make religion a stepping stone to preferment? Yet until it shall be proved that wicked men would not thus pervert a true religion, this perversion of Christianity, is no argument against its divinity. Is gold less valuable because it has been counterfeited; or, because *Thomas Paine* pretends to reason, is reason a useless faculty? If your bibles countenance hypocrisy, pride, and oppression, they are unworthy of your regard; but while they inculcate nothing but what is virtuous and praiseworthy, bind them to your hearts, faithfully follow the directions they give, and they will lead you to safety and happiness.

Another instance of modern sophistry is, to resolve religion into prejudice, and constantly use these terms as synonymous. This is a most popular stroke. It is infallible with men of weak minds, who would be thought *philosophers*. The very sound of vulgar prejudices frightens them out of that pittance of judgment which was theirs by original inheritance. But is this a fact, that mankind are biased in favor of doctrines which stand opposed to all the strong, leading passions of the heart? Universal observation teaches, that we are apt to be prepossessed in favor of what we wish to be true; but the modern doctrine of prejudices, contradicts this observation: it represents mankind as unaccountably disposed to believe, in opposition to the dictates of reason, and the impulse of inclination.

That Voltaire, after writing forty volumes against Christianity, and spending twenty years in attempting to *"crush the wretch,"* should be tormented by prejudices in favor of religion, may appear credible to those who "believe in unbelief;" but in this, and many similar instances, every unbiased mind will see a superior power impressing the soul with an irresistible consciousness of Almighty justice.

Not the arguments in support in Christianity, but those of an opposite nature owe their influence to the power of prejudice. These deceivers are not unmindful of the opposition of the heart to the restraints of religion. On this principle, corruption of morals becomes an important part of their system. They studiously endeavor to inflame the passions of men, that the obligations of duty may become more irksome; and that the cause they wish to support, may find a more powerful advocate in the heart. Infidelity owes its strength, not to argument, but to feeling. An hundredth the part of the evidence which has been produced in support of the truth of Christianity, would determine every person's judgment, in all cases, where the inclinations had no influence.

My countrymen, suffer not the arts of sophistry, or your own passions, to rob you of that benign religion which was so dear to your ancestors, which supported them under their trials, rendered their names precious to posterity, and originated establishments so happy in their effects.

3rd. Consider the importance of having your public offices filled with men of virtue and religion. This is indeed included in the example of your ancestors; for they had the wisdom to discern, that none but those who were friends to religion, were friends to society; but the present alarming inattention to this subject, recommends it to more particular notice.

Are magistrates the ministers of God, and the representatives of the Supreme Ruler? Thus *Christians* are taught to consider them. When, therefore, a nation, nominally Christian, elect to these offices, men avowedly, or practically opposed to the Christian religion, is it not a public affront to the righteous Ruler of the universe? However casuists may determine this question, the aspect, which the election of such men has upon the interest of society, is in every respect highly unfavorable. A person of this description, may faithfully serve his country, or he may betray, or he may enslave it; what course he will take, depends merely on circumstances. A regard to reputation, and what is called the principles of honor, which might have an influence in smaller concerns, cease to operate when the high objects of ambition are presented to the mind. When a man of ambition comes within the reach of supreme power, its attraction overcomes the influence of those weaker motives, which, for a time, held him within the sphere of duty. In these circumstances men of principle only, such as was the Jewish MOSES, and the American WASHINGTON, and ADAMS, will remain in their proper orbit, superior to all attraction, but that of their country's good.

To pretend that a man destitute of the principles of religion, will be as likely to be faithful to the interests of his constituents, as the one of opposite character, is to deny that religion tends to the good of society. But have the oaths of office, a belief of the being and perfections of God, and of a future state of rewards and punishments, no influence to excite men to fidelity? We know they are nothing to him who believes, *that death is an everlasting sleep,* but they cannot fail to operate on every mind which is not past feeling.

It is futile to attempt to justify an inattention to the characters of those we elect to office, by pretending, that to serve the purposes of ambition, men may assume a character which does not belong to them. It is not easy for those who are objects of public notice, to conceal, for a long period, their ruling passion; and were suitable caution used, it is not probable that a deception would frequently take place. In any event, this cannot justify inattention to the subject. Shall we, with our eyes open, trust our dearest interests with a knave, because it is possible we may be deceived in the man we believe to be honest? Our utmost care to preserve our dwellings may prove ineffectual, but shall we therefore put fire to them?

When due care is taken to elect men of good principles to public offices, even if the electors are deceived in the man of their choice, the object is not wholly lost. The character of the Supreme Ruler is duly respected; the public suffrage is on the side of virtue, and virtuous men are countenanced; wickedness suffers a public frown, and the person elected, perceiving that he owed his advancement to a virtuous character, will be more careful to support such a character; and temptations to neglect, or betray his trust, will have less effect upon him; but when infidelity is no bar to promotion, or when virtue and religion are considered as of no importance in a public character, these restraints are removed, and every temptation operates with full force.

When men, destitute of the principles of religion, are raised to important public offices, the effect must be extremely pernicious, as it respects the interests of religion in society. You are not now to learn what influence examples, and especially the examples of the great, have on the general state of manners and society. The temper of such men will influence their manners. However they may adopt some of the forms of piety, from a regard to appearances, their immoral and Anti-Christian feelings, will give a complexion to their whole deportment.

I do not hesitate to say, that the man, with whom these considerations have no weight, is a stranger to the nature, excellence, and importance of Christianity, and has the heart of an infidel. You will not, my countrymen, unless you are fatally blinded to your own interests, suffer the glare of abilities, or the impulse of a party spirit, to allure you to commit the interests of your country to men, who are enemies to those principles which form the pillars of society.

Our inattention to the choice of public officers is highly criminal. Many entirely neglect the right of suffrage, while others bring forward the name which chance, or some more designing than themselves, presents to them. What should we say of a ruler who should make choice of his principal offices in the same careless and capricious manner? Neither an individual, nor a multitude, ought to have the disposal of the affairs of a nation, who is not more attentive to its interests. Greater electioneering zeal is not, indeed, necessary than appears in some parts of our country; but it is fervently to be wished, that this zeal were less under the impulse of party spirit, and that calm, dispassionate citizens would make it a more serious object to discover, and introduce into public offices, characters, whose election might promise prosperity to their country.

4th. Beware of men, who seek to rob you of your liberties and religion, by flattering your passions, and by a pretended concern for your interests. This is not a new mode of deception, but, in common with other modes, has undergone a modern refinement. Marat, the greatest incendiary in France, Dr. Moore observes, "addressed the mob in the style of a lover to his mistress; and the motto of a Journal, which he published, was '*Ut rediat miseris, abeat fortuna superbis,*' that is, '*Take the money from the rich, that it may be restored to the poor.*'"

As a guard against the influence of ambitious, popular men, the Athenians provided the sentence of ostracism. Each citizen was required to write on a bone the name of the person, in his estimation, the most popular; and he whose name was found on the greatest number of bones, was banished from the Commonwealth, under the idea, that he had acquired an influence dangerous to the republic. However absurd in itself, and cruel in its operation, this practice was, it discovered a due sense of the danger arising, in a free government, from the ascendancy ambitious men may acquire, by flattering the populace, and gaining the direction of their passions. While there are corrupt, ambitious men, this kind of influence will exist, and will be principally found in those governments where its operation is most pernicious. Not, however, in ostracism, but in virtuous habits, and a watchful attention to the interests of the public, shall we find our safety from the arts of these insidious foes.

To confound the reputation which is the result of faithful services, and approved merit, with the popularity of an imposter, is as injurious to the public, as to individuals. The former is as beneficial, as the latter is destructive. A small degree of discernment, duly exercised, is generally sufficient to detect the insincerity of those who flatter but to destroy. If I may be indulged a quotation so unfashionable, I would say, that St. Paul has accurately described these deceivers; "They *zealously* affect you," says he, "but not *well;* yea, they would exclude you, that ye might *affect them.*"

The man who lives only for himself, while he pretends a deep concern for the interests of society; the fomenter of factions; the seeker of offices; the corrupter of morals; the avowed enemy of Christianity; the man who endeavors to irritate your mind, by representing necessary public expenses, as an act of oppression, and those restraints which the order of society requires, as tyrannical; in fine, he who addresses your passions, rather than your understandings, such men bear the genuine characteristics of imposters; and are either the deluded agents of a party, or have themselves designs which they wish to conceal, while they proclaim themselves the advocates of the rights of man.

5th. Attend to the sources from which you derive your political information. The disorganizers of Europe were not unmindful of the advantage to be derived to their cause from having public presses, and periodical publications, under their direction. There, however, a degree of caution was necessary, and an apprehension of consequences gave a check to the licentiousness of the press; but in the Unites States, this medium of imposition is, in a great measure, unembarrassed; and demands very serious attention. Excepting the salutary restraints imposed by the *Sedition Bill,* those who were disposed to foment divisions, excite jealousies, and disunite the people from their government, have had an opportunity of incessantly attacking the minds of the citizens with the grossest misrepresentations.

Evils of great magnitude have already originated from this source of mischief. Objects have been presented to the public, under every possible circumstance of distortion, and suspicions excited which were entirely groundless. It is an outrage upon common sense to pretend, that there has been any adequate cause for the clamors and opposition which have embarrassed the measures of the late administration. Could the citizens of the United States have an impartial view of their proceedings, it is to be presumed, that ninety-nine hundredths of the virtuous, enlightened part of the community, would cordially approve of what, by the influence of misrepresentation, many are now led to reprobate.

An effectual remedy for the abuses of the press has not yet been discovered, and perhaps, in a free government, no other remedy can be consistently resorted to then the virtue and good sense of the citizens; and this, we have reason to fear, will be but feeble indeed. The present state of the public mind is evidently calculated to increase, rather than diminish, this evil.

If, my countrymen, you will calmly and dispassionately inquire after truth, means of information are not wanting. If you give no encouragement to the numerous productions of the day, which are plainly dictated by a desire, not to inform your judgments, but to inflame your passions, they will cease; but while your minds are open to scurrility, calumnies, and falsehoods, they will abound. A spirit of party has given currency to many publications, from different quarters, which ought never to have seen the light. Truth is more injured than assisted, by an alliance with passion. Important truths are not, indeed, to be suppressed, because they may irritate the enemies of truth; but groundless aspersions, and needless provocations, should meet your pointed disapprobation, if the salvation of your country is dearer than the support of a party.

It is not the designs of these observations to dissuade you from an attention to public affairs. Your country needs, and has a right to demand, your vigorous efforts. It adds additional shade to the darkness of the present day, that, where the stimulus of party spirit does not operate, there is such a degree of torpor and inattention to a subject in which the happiness of millions is involved. A neglect of public interest must be viewed as criminal in any state of society, but more especially where the people claim to be the sources of honor and authority. But let your exertions be given to your *country,* not to a *party;* and being convinced that religion, morals, order, and a government of laws, are the pillars of your national prosperity and peace, let these have your firm and vigorous support.

6th. Renounce the Anti-Christian and irrational practice of "speaking evil of dignities." "Thou shalt not speak evil of the ruler of thy people," is one of those divine precepts which commends itself to every man's conscience by its evident propriety, and demands our attention as of prime importance to the order of society. It is an evil to which free governments are peculiarly exposed; and a strong propensity in human nature to this evil, has given an advantage to the disorganizers of the present day, which they have not neglected.

The impracticability of supporting the authority of the laws, and the energy of the government, when the executors of those laws, and the officers of that government, are objects of constant scurrility and abuse, must be obvious to every person of the least reflection. The experience we have had of this spirit among ourselves, is surely sufficient to satisfy us of its pernicious tendency; and under a change of administration, it is painful to see many indulging in the same spirit, which they have so justly reprobated in others. In the person, constitutionally invested with authority, we are to contemplate, not the *individual* whose election we once opposed, however reasonable and well founded that opposition may have been, but the *magistrate,* in supporting whom, on constitutional ground, we support the government of which he is the head.

Even when the public good requires, as doubtless it may require, that the character and conduct of public officers should be exposed, a solemn decency, and not a bitter and licentious spirit, still less a spirit of falsehood, ought to mark the transaction. Nor will the censurable parts of their conduct justify our withholding aid, countenance, and support in the due execution of their office.

7th. Seriously reflect upon the nature and tendency of secret societies. Weishaupt himself proposed the question, "Have you any idea of the power of secret societies?" It is obvious, at first view, that they are not friendly to the harmony and cordial union which are so desirable in every society. Should some of the children in a family form themselves into a secret club, exclude their brethren from their private meetings and confidence, and be often whispering their secrets, it is easy to foresee that an undue partiality among the confederated brethren, and jealousy, distrust, and alienation of affection on the other part, would be the natural consequences. The effects will be similar and equally certain, though they may be less visible, in larger societies. From the notorious tendency of such combinations, many weighty and interesting objections were made to the establishment of the order of the *Cincinnati;* but the development of the mysteries of Illuminism, has given additional weight to these arguments, and placed, in glaring light, the dangerous tendency of exclusive confederacies.

I am not insensible that these remarks criminate, in a degree, the order of Masonry. The respect I feel for many gentlemen of this order, among my acquaintance, who, I doubt not, entered the society with pure intentions, and yet remain free from this contamination; and my belief of the uncorruptness of the New England lodges in general, have made it, to me, an ungrateful task to relate the dark designs to which their order, after so long preserving its luster, has been subjected. I can assure them that views, to which every private consideration must yield, have been my sole inducement to undertake this duty. This, in the minds of those of the order whose approbation is most to be valued, I doubt not will appear a sufficient apology. To these candid Masons I hesitate not to say, that to me, a suspension at least, of Masonic operations, appears to be a measure, which the safety of society, in its present state, recommends; and it is difficult to conceive how any person, who admits the truth of the foregoing statements, can differ from this idea. It is the sentiment of many respectable Masons; and several lodges in Germany have actually closed their proceedings, on this principle. It is with pleasure I transcribe an extract from a Masonic oration on such an occasion, hoping, that the example and the sentiment, will have their due influence.

"Brethren and Companions, give free vent to your sorrow; the days of innocent equality are gone by. However holy our mysteries may have been, the lodges are now profaned and sullied. Brethren, and companions, let your tears flow; attired in your mourning robes attend, and let us seal up the gates of our temples, for the profane have found means of penetrating into them. They have converted them into retreats for their impiety, into dens of conspirators. Within the sacred walls they have planned their horrid deeds, and the ruin of nations. Let us weep over our *legions* which they have seduced. Lodges that *may serve* as hiding places for these conspirators must remain forever shut, both to us and every good citizen."*

He who thus sacrifices his amusements and pleasures to the interests of society, acquires a dignity beyond what the highest honors of Masonry can confer.

8th. Cheerfully submit to the restraints which the rules of religion and good order of society require. There are principles in the human heart which unwillingly endure control, and on these principles the disorganizers of the day place their chief dependence. They artfully endeavor to inflame the passions, to awaken a desire of forbidden objects and gratification, and then exhibit the restraints of religion and government, as tyrannically opposing enjoyment.

This is the true import of *liberty and equality*, as the words are used by modern imposters. The abuse to which these terms are liable is obvious; for, when once unlawful passions are excited, it becomes an easy task to persuade men that whatever checks those inclinations, is an abridgement of their natural liberty; and when, in this way, a popular torrent is formed, in vain religion, order, justice, or humanity oppose their restraints. *Liberty* is a vague term, nor do these men wish to define it; they wish to have men

---

* Barruel's Memoirs, Vol. IV. p. 63.

feel that they are injured by whatever opposes their inclinations, and when they have instilled into them this sentiment
of sedition, it is easy to render men hostile to all the restraints which religion and social order impose. This is the
liberty which Illuminism has actively propagated. Modern
philosophers have discovered, that the laws of modesty
impose an unjust restraint on the freedom of the fair sex;
that the subjugation which children are required to yield to
their parents, is an unreasonable usurpation; and the law
which obliges married people to live together, after their
affections for each other are alienated, is tyrannical.

But you, my countrymen, do not wish for this kind of
liberty. The glory of your constitution is, that it preserves
the citizens in the free enjoyment of their natural rights,
under the protection of equal laws and impartial justice.
You wish to have your lives, property, and privileges, both
civil and religious, preserved to you: Guard then those of
your neighbors; for know, that the moment the enclosures
which protect their rights are broken down, yours are no
longer secure. Whatever weakens the force of moral and
religious obligations; whatever lessens the restraints, already
sufficiently weak, which the laws impose on the unruly
passions of men, proportionally exposes the lives, liberties,
and property of the quiet part of the community to the
depredations of the lawless.

One of the most surprising effects attending to the
disorganizing principles of the day, is, that men of property
should be induced to give support to a system which
destroys the barriers by which property is protected. That
some few, who wish to acquire influence, and mount into
places of honor and trust, should adopt these violent means
to "burst open the doors" leading to the emoluments of
office, is not, indeed, strange; but the quiet, unambitious
citizen, whose utmost wish is to preserve the fruit of his

labor and exertion, must be completely duped not to perceive, that he exposes to the greatest hazard what he is principally desirous to preserve. Pleased with the idea of saving a few shillings, necessary for the defense of his property, he exposes the whole.

In the same absurd manner do *they* reason, who conceive that the perfection of liberty consists in unbounded indulgence. Extremes are said to meet and produce similar effects. This maxim applies to the present case. When people grow weary of subjecting their passions to necessary restraints, a state of disorder and faction ensues. Some popular leader, improving his ascendancy over the divided, distracted multitude, erects a despotism; and, flattering their passions, he at length establishes his authority on a surer basis.

Read the truth in the history of ancient Greece and Rome. See it verified in modern France. Advancing, in their own opinion, to the very pinnacle of liberty and equality, we see them suddenly reduced to a state of complete vassalage. The discerning part of the nation were not deceived, but weary of a liberty which left no security to their lives or property, they acquiesced in the usurpation of the Chief Consul: This is the natural and unavoidable consequence of licentious indulgences. Hearken not then, my countrymen, to those, who endeavor to render you dissatisfied with the restraints of religion, or the expenses necessary for the maintenance of useful institutions, and the support of good government.

To the Clergy

A S this subject is particularly interesting to the AMERICAN CLERGY, I beg leave to present it to them in a point of view, in which it appears to me of peculiar importance.

Fathers and Brethren,

W H I L E I see with pleasure your exertions in opposition to the prevailing infidelity, permit me to direct your attention to a temptation, by which, as we learn from the preceding historical sketches, the German divines were ensnared, viz. that of attempting to reconcile infidels to the gospel, by reducing it to their taste; either by explaining away, or keeping out of sight, its offensive peculiarities. From the foregoing recital it appears, that the second branch of Illuminism, the German Union, was grafted on a mutilated system of Christianity.

In the history of the Christian church, we are often reminded of the injuries Christianity has received from the attempts of its advocates to render the gospel palatable to its opposers. Upon this principle, first the Oriental, then the Platonic, afterward the Aristotelian, systems of philosophy became, in different ages, the standards for explaining the sacred writings; and the doctrines of Infinite Wisdom have been distorted into a compliance with those systems of human weakness and folly. Hence, also, arose the scheme of an hidden meaning, and mystical interpretation, so zealously adopted by Origen and others.

This doubtless has been sometimes done with a friendly design, but the consequences have always been unhappy; and unhappy they ever must be. Besides the impiety of the attempt, it is very obvious, that it is merely the corruptions, in these mutilated systems, with which infidels harmonize. Their hearts are no more reconciled to the *Gospel* than before; all the advantage resulting to Christianity consists in the external aid they afford the cause; and this is incomparably overbalanced by the injury done to the purity of its doctrines. Nor is even this aid now to be expected; for modern infidels, renouncing their former pretended respect for natural religion, have taken their proper ground, which is absolute atheism.

"This did not Paul." While fully sensible that the gospel he preached was, "a stumbling block to the Jew, and foolishness to the Greek," he complimented neither the one nor the other, either by adopting their sentiments, or relinquishing his own; but with a resolution worthy of the great defender of Christianity, determined, in the face of this opposition, to assert the doctrine of a crucified Savior; nay, as if foreseeing the indirect measures which some would take to recommend Christianity, he pronounces "him accursed who should preach another gospel," adding, that by *another gospel*, he meant the gospel of Christ perverted, or corrupted.

In this he conformed to the will of his Divine Master, who stated unalterably the terms of admission into his kingdom, declaring with the greatest solemnity, that unless they received the kingdom of God (the scheme of doctrines that he taught) with the meekness, and teachableness of little children, they should in no wise enter therein. It will not be pretended that he was unmindful of the opposition of the human heart to the doctrines he taught, but under a full view of that opposition, he demanded for them a ready reception, and the unequivocal submission of mankind. The triumph of the gospel is effected not by relinquishing its demands, in compliance with the corruptions and caprices of mankind, but in subduing the pride, enmity, and opposition of the heart, and "bringing into captivity every thought to the obedience of Christ."

I have thus, my countrymen, expressed my sentiments with the freedom which is *yet* one of the happy privileges of our country; and with the faithfulness which becomes one who sees his fellow men exposed to imminent dangers, I have never covered a paragraph, on any of the subjects here brought into view, by an anonymous publication. By this observation I mean not to criminate, in the least degree, those gentlemen, who, in this way have enlightened and instructed the public; but it is most agreeable to my feelings, especially in the present circumstances, to make myself responsible to the public, for my opinions on these subjects.*

Considering the spirit of the times, a meaning and design will doubtless be attributed to the writer which never entered his mind. With respect to himself, this is a circumstance of trifling consequence; as it respects the success of his labors, he is desirous to remove every obstacle; and would therefore observe, that nothing has been introduced into this work but what, it was conceived, would serve to give weight to the directions suggested in this address. In your attention to these sentiments consists your strength.

---

* Had the proper names of the authors been affixed to all the publications of the day, it is to be presumed that the clergy would be found chargeable with a small proportion of those which have been so liberally palmed upon them without the least evidence, and plainly with a design to injure their characters.

Your enemies must draw you from this ground before they can prevail. BELIEVE IN THE LORD YOUR GOD, SO SHALL YOU BE ESTABLISHED; BELIEVE HIS PROPHETS, SO SHALL YE PROSPER.*

---

* 2 Chronicles, xx. 20.

Conclusion

PAINFUL has it been to me, and no less so, I presume, to the reader, to traverse these regions of moral death, and to contemplate the direful effects produced by torrents of corruption, flowing from the fullness of the human heart. Gladly would I relieve his mind, and my own, with brighter prospects and more cheerful scenes; and such present themselves to him who meekly receives the instructions of his Maker, and surveys futurity with an eye of faith. By this light we discover, that the plan of Providence, however complicated its operations, is but one; having for its benevolent object, the production of order out of confusion, of good from evil. Under the government of Infinite Wisdom and love, this consoling truth is exemplified in numberless instances, from the plant, which owes its vigor to putrefaction, to the increasing purification the good man derives from conflicts and sufferings; and from thence to the cross of a Savior which gave life to the world. If we admit this prime truth, we need not a spirit of prophecy to foresee, that these efforts of infidelity will prepare the way for, and hasten its destruction: That the convulsions excited by these disorganizers will (but not in the way which they predict, nor according to their intentions) purify its constitution, and introduce an healthier state into society: That all the attempts which have been made to destroy the foundations of moral obligation, and the evidences of Christianity, will eventually establish the one, and confirm the other.

Is it asked when this happy era will commence? Not perhaps in this theorizing generation; not while men's heads are filled with the idea of erecting a peaceful, happy republic upon the basis of atheism. But the time will come, when wisdom will resume her seat, and man will submit to be taught by experience, and by his Maker. Then will his ear be opened to the lessons of wisdom, to the demonstrations of truth, which the history of the present period affords.

Would it be extravagant to assert, that the collected history of all ages and nations, sacred history excepted, does not furnish so much important and useful instruction, as will probably be derived from the events which have come into view within the last sixty years? In the period referred to, we have been presented with what may be considered, as a course of experimental lectures on religion, morals, and the interests of society; in which many important principles and truths have received a clear illustration, and been demonstrated to the senses.

In many excellent treatises has Christianity been defended, and the tendency of infidelity, in its influence on the mind, and on society, held up to the public; but as abstract reasonings make but a faint impression on the great body of mankind, infidels, have confidently denied the charges brought against them, and the justness of the conclusions drawn from their sentiments. Infidels have formed the minority in every society; they were therefore naturally led to plead for *toleration*. Their principles were under a continual check, and a regard to reputation and personal safety, induced a compliance with the customs and manners of the age. In proof of the importance of religion to a civil community, the advocates of Christianity appealed to the state of society in heathen nations; but this did not amount to a fair experiment; for the heathens were not infidels. The scattered rays of revelation, collected by their philosophers, produced something like a system of religion, which, however inadequate to the principal purposes of religion, had a happy effect on society and morals.

Infidelity never before appeared in her proper character. Infidels, formerly, spake much of virtue and religion, applauded the morality of the gospel, and affected to admire many of its doctrines. Lord Herbert calls "the Christian, the best religion." Lord Bolingbroke represents "Christianity as a most amiable and useful institution, and that its natural tendency is to promote the peace and happiness of mankind." It was plead by the advocates of Christianity, that whoever had any real love to moral beauty could not but embrace the gospel; but deists denied the truth of this assertion, and to support their argument, were perpetually proclaiming the beauty of virtue and natural religion. But now it appears that all this was a mere finesse, adapted to conceal the fatal tendency of their opinions. Infidelity, confiding in her strength, and the increasing number of her advocates, has now laid aside her mask, and we have seen her in France, fierce, cruel, unjust, oppressive, abandoned and profligate, as she is; rejecting those moral precepts she once professed to admire, proudly assuming entire independence, and ranking the sovereign of heaven with the tyrants of the earth.

We have grounds to expect, that the genuine tendency, both of infidelity and Christianity, as they respect society, will be fully and undeniably demonstrated. It is undoubtedly a part of the scheme of Providence, to lay open the human heart, and to prove important truths by convincing experiments. Were mankind duly impressed with that view of the tendency of infidelity, which late events have exhibited, it would afford a rational hope that its reign would soon cease; but while so many remain unconvinced, there is reason to fear its more deplorable prevalence, before the dawning of that happy day, when Christianity, infusing its benign influence into every heart, shall produce permanent peace, and the precious fruits of universal love.

FINIS.

Printed in the United States
1110900002B